Frankfurt
THROUGH THE CENTURIES

GEORGE G. WYNNE

Second Edition
edited by
HEIDI ANDRIEN & ALBERT E. SCHROCK

PUBLISHED BY WALDEMAR KRAMER

FRANKFURT

To Mary
who gave me a son
while I put together a book

Second Edition 1975
© 1957 Dr. Waldemar Kramer, Frankfurt am Main
ISBN 3-7829-0167-3
Printed in Germany
W. Kramer & Co., Frankfurt am Main

TABLE OF CONTENTS

A Frankfurt American, or an American Frankfurter by his own choice, originally wrote this book. Dr. George G. Wynne lived in Frankfurt for several years. His journalistic instinct, his gift as an author and his tremendous thirst for knowledge became the one motive for this book about Frankfurt; his dedication to the city on the Main and his desire for a bridge between the distant United States and the German metropolis, and many friendly contacts to Frankfurters, the other.

The revised version presents many contemporary additions. But remaining still is the special emphasis on those events and institutions in Frankfurt of particular interest to the visitor from abroad. From the "Address of Sympathy from the Free German-Americans to the Revolutionary Assembly" in the Paulskirche, from the origin of the foundation of Pennsylvania in Frankfurt, from the millions of dollars credit for the American Civil War, the course of history is traced on to the liberation of Frankfurt from fascism by US troops. And therein even a native Frankfurter such as I can learn many new and interesting details.

But also the individuality of Frankfurt, the unequivocal character of a liberated city with tradition and independance becomes evident. Sachsenhausen, the Zoo, the Palm Garden and many other typical Frankfurt attractions are not only described, but the personal impressions of the editor are conveyed. The eminent history of Frankfurt as the electoral and coronation city of the emperors of the Holy Roman Empire of the German Nation, as the seat of the first German parliament, encounter us in word and picture. And finally, and this seems important to me, the picture of present day Frankfurt as a European metropolis with world-wide influence is painted. An excellent portrait, it appears to me.

RUDI ARNDT
Lord Mayor of the City of Frankfurt

Frankfurt am Main,
July 1975

FOREWORD TO THE FIRST EDITION

When U.S. High Commissioner John J. McCloy to whom our city is deeply indebted for his energetic support of our reconstruction activities in the difficult early years, opened the Frankfurt Fall Fair of 1949, he coined the excellent expression that the name of our city had become synonymous with the concept of freedom the world over.

May this little book, written with affection for Frankfurt by Dr. George G. Wynne obtain the grateful readers it deserves.

In doing so it will live up to its purpose, affording proof of Frankfurt's reputation as a free and cosmopolitan city as recognized in the words of the former High Commissioner.

Dr WALTER LEISKE
Mayor of the City of Frankfurt

Frankfurt am Main,
October 1957

Notes to the Second Edition

This book makes no claims to be a complete history of Frankfurt. Instead, it tries to provide a skeleton of the history and the significance of Frankfurt through the centuries, and a few vignettes of interest to the reader.

The revision of the first edition in the spring of 1975 seemed at first glance to be a simple enough task, merely the matter of updating a few statistics and adding a section on the last 20 years of Frankfurt history. But with each interview, with each telephone call to establish or confirm a fact, it became apparent that a city such as Frankfurt can no more be described accurately by statistics than a man can be. For a city is a living entity, with its own personality which is influenced by internal factors and external pressures, and which is constantly changing.

Hopefully, these glimpses into the Frankfurt of the past and the present, as seen from the perspective of 1975 will provide the reader an impression of this cosmopolitan city.

Many thanks to the individuals who assisted in the revision of the book — especially to Mr. Robert Harlan, the American Consul General of Frankfurt, whose personal interests, enthusiasm and knowledge of the history of Frankfurt, as well as the information made available from the archives of the Consulate, greatly assisted the accomplishment of this project. Also thanks to the officials of the city of Frankfurt, whose willing cooperation turned the routine and often times tedius research into a pleasure. Also, special thanks go to Col. Douglas G. Waters, whose personal interest in the project provided the impetus necessary to take it beyond the idea stage.

Heidi Andrien   Albert E. Schrock

INTRODUCTION

One day, after helping to arrange a city hall reception, I heard the head of a visiting group of artists reply to the Mayor as he accepted a framed etching of Frankfurt's historic Roemerberg: "We are happy to take this wonderful gift back with us. We are going to hang it where all our visitors will be able to see it. You see many people when they hear the word Frankfurt, think only of sausages, but this etching will convince them that it's also a great city." That morning, I resolved to write this book. Its main aim is to prove that Frankfurt stands for more than a sausage.

In doing so, the little volume hopes to serve a useful purpose for the many temporary residents and English-speaking visitors to the city who are likely to tread on historic terrain or walk past fascinating happenings of the past and present without knowing they are really there. The old Frankfurt has been largely obliterated, the new has not yet found final form. In this period of change the hasty visitor may fail to discover the historic heartbeat of the city and dismiss it as merely a modern collection of people, cars and buildings in many ways reminiscent of a medium-sized American city. But the steel and glass buildings cover the footfalls of a hundred generations. In centuries past, the ritual center of an empire in which the sun would not set, today the aerial gateway to a continent, Frankfurt has seen splendor and high living, wars and revolution, occupation armies ranging from ancient Rome to modern North America with the Swedes and the French thrown in for good measure. Pestilence stalked the city and kings held their court here, the lanes of commerce intersected, creating Europe's financial dynasties and bringing to Frankfurt goods of the Orient, silks, jewels and rare spices at a time when Columbus was still contemplating how to raise funds for his next voyage. Intermittent personal contact with the new world was started by this land-locked community as early as the 1550s when Frankfurt explorer Hans Staden became chieftain of Brazil Indians and the 1680s when Franz Daniel Pastorius representing the Frankfurt Land Company, founded Germantown, Pennsylvania while Frankfurt's native son Jacob Leisler became the first governor of New York.

More so than most cities in Germany, Frankfurt has enjoyed a tradition of civic rights, self-reliance and self-government. The fact that the community has been run according to their rights by elected city fathers, instead of the representatives of some distant king, created a fierce civic pride and a community spirit responsible in the same measure for outstanding public buildings as for the attitude of judging a man by his worth rather than his birth. Frankfurt's late great Lord Mayor Walter Kolb used to finger his heavy chain of office to draw assurance from the pledge of the free city that encircles the heraldic eagle. It reads: 'Strong in Law' and the life of Mayor Kolb gives ample proof that the best citizens of Frankfurt bowed only before God and the moral law. Weakened by persecution and imprisonment under the Nazis he died in 1956 after ten constructive years in office. The present city administration carries on his work in the tolerant and hospitable manner characteristic of the best in Frankfurt's tradition of public service.

Anxious to have their American friends and visitors feel at home in the city, they asked the writer to try and interpret Frankfurt's history and its links with the new world across the barrier of language and living habits.

Steeped in the comforts of housing projects, shopping centers and tourist facilities that conveniently re-create an American atmosphere, it takes something of an effort and a little ambition to stalk around the city and explore what makes it tick. But the experience is rewarding and I hope that the following pages might help give a new dimension to familiar streets and buildings. If in the process they point to new sights, help build understanding as well as memories, they will have been well worth doing.

I am deeply indebted to Mayor Dr. Walter Leiske and the City of Frankfurt for the genuine interest taken in this work and the cooperation helpfully extended by the Historical Museum, the municipal archives and libraries. Stadtrat Dr. Altheim and Director Arnold Weck in the city administration made it possible to assemble between these covers events and faces long since departed from the scene.

Special thanks go to Dr. Waldemar Kramer, a dedicated publisher and fine human being whose more than 100 volumes of *Frankfurteristika* supplied most of the source material. His encouragement and expert advice on fact-finding and picture selection helped speed the book to its completion.

Frankfurt am Main 1957   GEORGE G. WYNNE

SPOTLIGHTS ON HISTORY

Stone-age hatchets dating from the third millenium B. C., bronze-age swords and jewelled hair pins, iron necklaces and ornaments of the Celts are the earliest finds of the Frankfurt region. Hill-shaped grave mounds in the city forest near the present day site of Rhein Main airport testify to the funeral customs of the Celts whose culture merged with that of the Roman legions sent to colonize the conquered areas deep in Teuton territory. Protected against floods from the Main river which in those days washed half way up to the Roemerberg during high water season, the 14th Roman legion built a small settlement on Cathedral Hill connected by river boats and overland routes with the larger communities of Moguntiacum, as Mainz was then called after the Celtic sun God Mogus, and Nida, a Roman settlement just north of Frankfurt on the site of present day Heddernheim. The Roman legions who settled the land as farmer-soldiers, much in the manner of the latter day Russian cossacks frozen at imperial command at the outer rims of the Empire, were sent to secure Rome's first line of defense against the North. When the border fortifications, called the Limes, were decisively breached in about 250 A. D., Teuton invaders swept across the Main valley, razing all Roman settlements in their path. The fleeing Romans threw the valuables they had to abandon into deep wells where they were unearthed during the last century—some 1600 years

Votive altar of Roman legionaires found in the Frankfurt area.

later—by Frankfurt archaelogists. A pillar, dated March 13, 240, dedicated to Jupiter and Juno by one C. Sedatius Stephanus, Decurion of the City of Taunensium and his family, was discovered in a well in Heddernheim in 1884. It is now in Frankfurt's prehistoric museum.

Ironically, a Roman votive altar was discovered as a part of the north wall of Frankfurt's cathedral. It was probably used as a building stone and has been placed by its inscription in the period just before 280, when it was erected "to Mithras, the unconquered God, by the first cohort of the Sequanians commanded by Sextilius Primus, captain of the 22nd Legion under the Emperor Commodus."

No record survives from the succeeding five hundred years other than the historical conclusion implicit in the City's name Franconofurd, the place of old where the Franks forded the river. In the battles between Germanic tribes, the Franks drove out the Alemans who displaced the Romans. Around 500 A. D., Chlodwig, King of the Franks, consolidated his empire after driving the Alemans across the river into South Western Germany, and embraced Christianity in a ceremony held at Reims. Church records note that in the 8th century the Main valley was added to the bishopric of Mainz by Saint Boniface.

When Charlemagne called the mighty of the realm to Frankfurt in 794 to accept the submission of Bavaria's Duke Tassilo, the city already appears as the imperial residence and is referred to as a celebrated spot by the chronicler who has left us the first recorded mention of the "locus celeber, qui dicitur Franconofurd." The imperial palace was already a magnificent building and Charlemagne's son, Ludwig the Pious added new wings and service buildings during his frequent and extensive residence in the palace in the 26 years of his reign from 814 to 840. It was here that he held two imperial councils and celebrated the birth of his son Charles, who became known in history as Charles the Bald, first king of France. After World War II, excavations for the foundations of

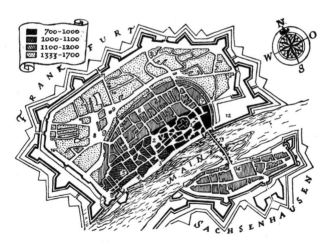

A thousand years of Frankfurt's growth.

new buildings on the site of the old city confirmed what archaeologists had long suspected: the exact location of Charlemagne's palace between Cathedral Hill and Roemerberg. Charlemagne's grandson, Ludwig the German, picked Frankfurt as his capital when he inherited the territories north of the Rhine, calling his empire East Franconia and the city "The Principal Seat of the Eastern Realm". He lived there until his death in 876.

The loose confederation of sovereign states, known as the Holy Roman Empire of the German Nation, which critical historians and philosophers have termed neither Holy nor Roman, nor indeed an Empire, began with the reign of Otto the Great, who had himself crowned by the Pope in Rome in 962. For nearly 600 years all German emperors followed this custom until Charles V, who abdicated his throne in 1556 and spent his remaining years in the seclusion of a Spanish monastery.

THE IMPERIAL RITUAL

Shoes from all over the world today shuffle across the polished floor where the crowned heads of the Holy Roman Empire once dined in imperial splendor. Their owners' muted talk in many tongues is absorbed by walls that witnessed the highlights of European history for the past 600 years.

For it was here that the newly-elected emperors dined on a raised dais in the majesty of the office bestowed upon them by the electors of the realm. Starting with Maximilian II in 1562, the emperors presided over the coronation banquet in this room. Even before, the nearby cathedral had served as the site of the emperors' election by the spiritual and temporal Lords of the Realm, a custom dating back to 1152, when Frederick Barbarossa became the first of 24 German emperors elected in Frankfurt. This famed "Red Beard" of medieval history drowned in 1189 during a river crossing while leading the third Crusade together with Richard the Lionhearted of England and Philip of France.

The Golden Bull of Charles IV, issued over 600 years ago in 1356, confirmed for all time Frankfurt's position as the electoral city of the Holy Roman Empire. Named after the gold capsule which encloses the imperial seal, the parchment document has survived the centuries without a scratch and remains to this day the most prized possession of the city's archives. The Bull minutely prescribes the electoral ritual noting that by custom from

The Great Seal of the Holy Roman Empire affixed to the Golden Bull.

time immemorial, Frankfurt had been the electoral city, Aachen the city of the coronation, and Nuremberg the place for the holding of the first council by the newly elected monarch. This constitutional certification of prevailing custom points to the rulers of the Franks as the first of the German kings. Even earlier documents, including a legal manuscript by an Augsburg cleric dating from 1275, note that the new king by virtue of his election, loses the law of his clan and his native land, and is required to govern the realm according to the legal precepts of the Franks, the so-called Salic Law.

For many centuries, imperial ritual in Frankfurt took its course down to the last detail as specified in the docu-

The Imperial Cathedral of Frankfurt after an etching by Salomon Kleiner, 1738.

Coronation of Emperor Joseph II in the Frankfurt cathedral, 1764.
(Painted by Martin van Meytens. Schoenbrunn Castle, Vienna.)

Traditional festivities on the Roemerberg during the coronation of Joseph II in 1764. (Painted from memory by Martin van Meytens. The canvas shows the Roemer buildings disproportionately elongated and a spire of St. Nicholas that bears little resemblance to the original.)

Frankfurt panorama in 1620. Etching by Matthaeus Merian.

ment of Charles IV "by the Grace of God, Roman Emperor, Protector of the Realm, King of Bohemia." The fiction of succession to the glory that was Rome, was maintained by the German kings to provide legality by association and the divine right to govern with the approval of the Catholic Church, and found its symbolic expression in the Gold Seal affixed to the Bull. The seal bears the inscription: 'Rome, the capital of the world, holds the reins of the globe.' A likeness of the emperor with the titles, robes and symbols of office is embossed on the obverse of the seal.

According to the Golden Bull, the election of the Holy Roman Emperor and German King was the prerogative of the three spiritual and four temporal Lords of the Realm. These were the Archbishops of Mainz, Trier, and Cologne; the Count Palatine of the Rhine, the Duke of Saxony, the Margrave of Brandenburg, and the King of Bohemia. When the time comes to elect a sovereign, the bull specifies, the Archbishop of Mainz is to invite the other electors to appear within a period of three months in Frankfurt or to dispatch to the electoral city their authorized emissaries. The retinue of each elector or his ambassador is to be not more than 200 mounted men, not more than 50 of them armed. The bull not only puts up safeguards against undue pressure, it also stipulates that an elector who fails to appear in Frankfurt or to be properly represented, loses his vote. It calls upon the citizens of the electoral city to protect the lords of the realm and their following from any enemies whatsoever even in case of strife among the electors themselves. No persons other than the electors and their authorized followings are to be permitted

The seven electors of the realm
deliberating on the choice of Henry VII as Holy Roman Emperor in 1308.

inside the city gates during the electoral period. Strangers found in the city are to be expelled; strict observance of these regulations is enjoined upon the citizens and the council of Frankfurt on pain of loss of their traditional privileges and freedoms. In the ritual language of the Bull the electors are charged with celebrating a Holy Mass in the Church of St. Bartholomew—the present day cathedral—prior to their deliberations on the choice of the new emperor in order that "the Holy Ghost may illuminate their hearts and infuse in their minds the light of its power, so that they might choose a good and capable man to be Roman King and future emperor for the benefit of all Christendom."

Negotiations preceding the elections of the emperor often ran over a period of months during which time

Emperor Henry VII
is placed upon the altar in the Frankfurt Cathedral following his election.

Frankfurt was the scene of costly displays by the various ambassadors, state dinners, fire-works, and the pomp and circumstance of pageantry. The wealthy patricians who were running the city were quick to realize the advantage of its special status. A few years after the promulgation of the Golden Bull, Charles IV delegated the privilege of appointing the mayor of the City to the City Council itself, thus Frankfurt became a 'Free Imperial City' responsible directly to the emperor, a status it maintained until its annexation by Prussia in 1866. All through the Middle Ages, the City Council, composed of the landed aristocracy, wealthy merchants, and representatives of the guilds, picked the mayor from among its ranks and governed the city in an oligarchy of the upper forty joined together in powerful family clans.

The weeks and months that led up to the climactic election, and since 1562, followed by the coronation of the emperor, provided a high spot in the life of each generation. An Englishman, Sir John Reresby, has left us an account describing the entry of foreign ambassadors during the electoral meetings leading up to the choice of Leopold I. These deliberations lasted nearly a year until July 1658, with the coronation ceremonies on the first of August.

Reresby writes: "The ambassadors entered the city with no less pomp and retinue than their masters, and they were received by Frankfurt with the same solemn ritual. The envoy of the King of Hungary arrived the same day we came to the city, he brought with him 15 carriages each of them drawn by six horses, also 9 baggage cars with their precious contents covered by velvet saddle cloth and blankets; these cars too were drawn by teams of six horses each, followed by 15 mounted servants and several ambassadors. He was met by the mayor, the head of the City Council and all its members, several leading citizens and the city militia. With standards flying and the music of drums and bugles, they escorted the ambassador to the official residence selected for him by the city.

"The most brillant entrance was staged by the Duke of Grammont, Peer and Marshal of France, and the Lord of Lyonne, who arrived as emissaries of the French King. They were escorted into the city by the mayor and prominent citizens; behind them came 26 pack mules carrying coffers and boxes covered with gold and silver-trimmed velvet cloth, their precious border ten inches wide. Then came 22 pages in gold and silver-embroidered liveries with plumed hats, silk stockings and fur-lined coats, after them 80 gentlemen in the employ of the ambassadors, all richly-clad and well-mounted, then the personal horses of the ambassadors, 12 in number, followed by 26 messengers in liveries only slightly less pretentious then those of the pages, and finally the ambassadors themselves with a few personal servants. This procession was followed by twelve carriages lined in red silk or velvet, trimmed with gold and silver tassels and each drawn by teams of twelve horses. Four baggage cars drawn by four horses each, adorned like the others with velvet saddle cloth, closed the ambassadorial train."

When the great day dawned the formal election ceremony began with the incessant pealing of the so-called storm bells, whose ringing was reserved to warn citizens of fires or other natural catastrophes and armed attack against the city. When the storm bell sounds on the hallowed day of election, an ancient edict enjoins citizens 'to stop in their tracks and offer solemn prayers that the newly-crowned Roman Emperor shall govern with God's help for the benefit of Christendom'. As the bells pealed, the electors assembled at the Roemer to be cloaked in their robes of state and walk in stately procession across Roemer square to the north portal of St. Bartholomew's. They mount their pews in the electoral chapel, the Protestants among them withdraw into conclave where they are joined by the Lords Spiritual, the Archbishops of Mainz, Cologne and Trier, following the Mass to the Holy Ghost. The formal conclave ends with the oath of allegiance to the new sovereign by the electors and solemn declarations of policy by the new ruler taken down and certified by the notaries present.

The proclamation of the new King likewise takes place in the electoral chapel. From there the ruler accompanied by the electors returns to the nave of the Cathedral. He kneels before the main altar. Prayers and liturgical chants set in. The electors lift the new emperor and seat him atop the altar. A festive Te Deum joined in by all the mighty of the realm assembled for the electoral services, closes the church ceremonies.

Proceedings on the day of coronation begin with the delivery of the imperial symbols of authority, the crown, scepter, orb and the sword of Charlemagne by the emissaries of Aachen and Nuremberg. They are deposited on the altar of the cathedral. The Roman king is then met by the Lords Temporal and conducted into the cathedral were the three Archbishops, Lords Spiritual of the realm, are waiting. An auspicious reign is implored by a solemn mass; the King then sheds his wordly robes and kneels with the Archbishops before the tabernacle. He is asked to swear as a devout Christian that he will act as protector of the Church, guardian of the laws, augmentor of the Empire, that he will aid and shelter widows and orphans, and pay due homage to the Pope in Rome as the representative of Christ on earth. The ritual proceeds after the king's vow, with the nobles swearing obedience and submission. Now the King's head, chest, hands, and right arm are anointed. He withdraws into the sacristy to be helped into the heavy coronation robes which date back to the Norman rulers of Italy in the eleventh and

Emperor Leopold I
shown with the imperial crown, orb and scepter at his coronation in 1658.

twelfth century. Upon his re-appearance by the altar the sovereign is girded with the sword of Charlemagne; the imperial ring, scepter and orb are handed him.

The coronation ceremony then reaches its climax. The Archbishops of Mainz, Cologne and Trier, Lords Spiritual of the realm, jointly place on the head of the sovereign the crown of the Holy Roman Empire fashioned in 962 in Rome for the coronation of Otto the Great. Again the king vows to rule for the greater glory of God; the mass resumes and the new sovereign is conducted to the throne-chair of Charlemagne placed for the occasion in the south transept of the cathedral. The coronation ceremony is concluded as the nobles file past to offer their homage and the emperor raises to knighthood selected officials of the Empire.

The long awaited public celebration now gets under-way. Across a wooden boardwalk specially constructed for the occasion, covered with cloth in the imperial colors, the procession wends its way from the cathedral to the Roemer for the coronation banquet in the imperial chamber. Courtiers, counsellors and knights, drummers and heralds, dukes and princes precede the three electors of Trier, Palatinate and Brandenburg who carry the symbols of imperial authority before the emperor. In the center of the procession, the new sovereign walks in a stately measured gait under a canopy of yellow silk embroidered with the black, double-headed imperial eagle carried by the envied city-councillors of Frankfurt. The other four electors walk behind the canopy followed by clerics, court officials, and mounted clerks of the exchequer who throw to the crowds the newly-struck coronation coins of gold and silver.

No sooner has the procession disappeared inside the Roemer than a wild scramble ensues for the cloth and wood of the boardwalk over which the dignitaries had just walked to keep their feet clear of the mud and dirt of unpaved Roemerberg square. While the three electors of Saxony, Brandenburg and the Palatinate return to perform their hereditary ceremonial functions as marshal, steward and butler, the crowd mills in respectful distance around the wooden shed in which an entire ox is slowly roasting on a spit, the fountain of justice which spouts red wine and white for the occasion and the mound of oats for the emperor's horse placed on one side of the square. After the Duke of Saxony has put a measure of oats in a silver vessel, Brandenburg has brought a silver water pitcher, bowl and towel, the Palatine has cut the first choice morsel of beef, called the Kaiserstueck, from the roasted ox, and the King of Bohemia, as hereditary wine steward, has collected a ceremonial goblet of white and red to compete with the choice vintages on the Emperor's table, all is given over to the crowds. From the windows of the Roemer and the surrounding houses the imperial retinue, wealthy visi-

The "Black Star"

25

tors and citizens of Frankfurt watched the mad scramble. Windows of the timbered patrician houses bordering the square fetched a high price from well-to-do merchants and craftsmen who flocked to Frankfurt from all parts of Germany. At the coronation of Leopold II in 1790, for instance, the owner of the "Black Star", a Roemerberg house with 52 windows, earned the equivalent of 6000 dollars in a single day. In the jostling for the coveted trophies, black eyes, bruises and rowdy practical jokes were the order of the day. In the jostling before the fountain, hardly anyone could enjoy the wine. As soon as a muscular burgher had managed to fight his way to the spout and fill a stoneware beaker, his neighbor would hit the vessel from below, splashing its contents all over the celebrants. Entire guilds likewise fought for the carcass of the oxen. The strong men of the butchers guild traditionally had to defend this prize against rival factions in pitched street battles. Black eyes and contusions also accompanied the distribution of coronation coins thrown to the crowd from the Roemer window.

Muffled curtains meanwhile kept the noise of the crowd below from the great ceremonial state banquet which went its measured course in the Kaisersaal, the imperial chamber of the Roemer. The Emperor, his back to the windows on the far end of the hall, sat on a raised dais, five steps above the floor, faced by Europe's most lavish table. Each elector ate at a separate table, three of them spaced along each wall, with the Archbishop of Trier in the middle of the hall facing the Emperor's dais. A five-tiered sideboard lined with precious dishes, goblets and containers stood next to the Emperor's table, a three-tiered sideboard behind each elector. Costly embroidered draperies hung from the walls, heavy silk curtains shut off the outside world. Court musicians played a stately tune from a small gallery over the entrance, and the meal proceeded in silence in a setting made slightly eery by the vacant tables of absent electors. Due to ill health, internal strife, or the perils of travel, one or more of the electors sometimes failed to appear at the coronation proceedings. Nevertheless in accordance with the ritual, the absent elector's table was set, the individual courses brought and cleared away uneaten, while the populace caroused outside, and the lesser nobles held their separate banquets in the various council chambers of the Roemer.

A brillant display of fireworks over the Main river capped the official festivities of coronation day. The night sky was lit by Roman candles ignited from the turrets of an artful wooden castle constructed atop a barge moored in the middle of the river.

With minor variations this procedure was followed down to the last coronation in 1792, when Francis II, 45th and last Roman Emperor, was elected and crowned in Frankfurt on the Main. When he renounced the crown of the Empire that had become a fiction through Napoleon's conquests, his portrait was the last to have found room in the 45 niches of the Kaisersaal. The city council had long worried how to accommodate the pictures of future emperors once the 45 niches of the Kaisersaal were filled.

Destiny took this concern from the city council. When the last niche was filled, the Empire crumbled.

The 'Welcome Pretzel' for foreign merchants at the Frankfurt Fair.

THE FAIRS

Few of the guests at the reception for foreign visitors given annually by the Frankfurt Fair know they are continuing an 800 year tradition when they bite into the oversize pretzels presented each of them as a gift of the city. The 'escort pretzel' as it appears today in its sanitary cellophane envelope is a direct descendant of the welcome offerings bestowed on foreign merchants traveling to the fairs from its earliest beginnings under imperial safe conduct guarantees. From a strictly local market in the days of Charlemagne, the fair evolved through the centuries to a focal point of international commerce, favored by its central location in the heart of Europe.

The primacy of the Frankfurt fairs was confirmed as early as 1240 when Emperor Frederick II issued letters of imperial protection to Italian merchants embarking on the arduous trip over the Alps to the great trading center. 'To all who shall see these presents' the documents read, 'and to the world at large, be it known that each and every one who travels to the fairs at Frankfurt is accorded our own and the Empire's special protection'. Frederick took time out from his wars against the Pope to sign the certificates of protection drawn up in his field headquarters outside Piacenza in Northern Italy. But even before this official deed of protection, Italian merchants had journeyed to Frankfurt bringing with them silks and velvets, tropical fruits, spices, weapons and jewelry. In Frankfurt they lived in houses named after them the 'Roemer', 'Milano' and 'Lateran'. The first of these names stuck on the house bought by the Council in 1405 and used as a city hall ever since.

For the convenience of foreign merchants and the profit of Frankfurt citizens, the houses around Roemerberg square were rented out for the storage of precious and perishable goods during the fair season. From the rents charged, some of the wealthier citizens constructed additional buildings purposely kept vacant for use as warehouses by major suppliers of foreign merchandise. Separate entrances to the different storage chambers in each building showed the outlines of different animal figures hewn into stone tablets to enable foreigners unfamiliar with language and surroundings to spot their location at a glance.

The Frankfurt fair on the Roemerberg, 1696.

Responding to the requests of citizens who found a single annual fair insufficient to cover the demand for goods, Emperor Ludwig the Bavarian in 1330 granted Frankfurt the privilege of holding a second annual fair during Lent. He designated both of them as official fairs of the Empire and decreed that no other town in Germany should establish similar trading enterprises in competition with Frankfurt. During the next five hundred years only one of the thousand scheduled fairs had to be cancelled, in the terrible year of 1635 during the Thirty Years' War.

Between the trade fairs and the book fairs, the latter as important to the intellectual life of the continent as the former to the economy of Europe, Frankfurt came to be known as 'the market of markets'. The virtues of the local fairs were extolled by authors and playwrights of many nations. Shakespeare had Shylock, the merchant of Venice, buy his precious diamonds at the fair in Frankfurt; Henri Etienne of France eulogized the book fair as 'the seat of Apollo and the Muses', in a Latin poem penned in 1574, and an Englishman named Thomas Coryat wrote in 1611: "Frankfurt's street of books excels by far St. Paul's Place in London, St. Jacob's street in Paris, the Merceria of Venice, and all that I saw in my travels." Coryat traveled the continent on foot following the Rhine downstream to Holland from its source in Switzerland.

"The central location of Frankfurt in the heart of Europe has predestined it for the fair as by divine providence", French printer Henri Etienne wrote in his Journals, "and its fame derives from the many other markets that flow into it".

A page of inventory records of the fall fair of 1492,
kept by Frankfurt wholesaler Wolf Blum.

By a quirk of fate, the record of goods shipped to Frankfurt from Venice by wholesaler Wolf Blum during the fall fair of 1492 has come down to us through the centuries. Blum's inventory clerk carefully penned his entries into the parchment log book of the trading house just at the time Christopher Columbus was busy discovering the continent whose products in later years wielded a decisive influence on the commerce of the old world.

Foreign merchants, attracted to Frankfurt either by trading opportunities or by religious persecutions in surrounding countries, brought new skills, new styles of building and a keen spirit of competition to the medieval city. Dutch Calvinist refugees displaced from their homeland by the intolerance of the country's Spanish Catholic rulers settled in Frankfurt in the 1550's. They were joined thirty years later by merchants fleeing from Antwerp after the conquest of their native city by Spanish general Alexander Farnese. The wealthy Dutch merchants who transferred their activities to Frankfurt were soon followed by a retinue of goldsmiths, diamond cutters, portrait painters and experts in decoration and manufacture of the delicate delftware. They introduced their flourishing industry to Frankfurt, producing here some of the finest examples of European crockery between 1666 and 1710. Fine examples of their 'Frankfurter Fayence Manufaktur' have been preserved in the city's historical museum.

The wealth brought by Dutch merchants to the city or quickly acquired here made the new settlers welcome in Frankfurt, but in religious matters the native Lutheran

The 'Fahrtor' at the Main river embankment, transfer point for trade fair goods during the Middle Ages. (Section of a painting by W. F. Hirt in the Frankfurt Historical Museum.)

The old city of Frankfurt (The Old Market) before its destruction in World War II. Left: Open air butcher's stalls — birthplace of the "Frankfurter" (sausage).

The Eschenheimer Tower. Drawing by Ph. Reinermann, 1841.

The north portion of the Roemerberg on market day after a painting by Chr. G. Schuetz d. A., 1754.

community was less than tolerant to the new Calvinist arrivals. Local restrictions on their religious services and petty chicaneries on the part of the Council drove the Dutch into transferring their congregation to the nearby village of Bockenheim. For centuries afterwards, the Lutheran city council even maintained an edict prohibiting Reformed and Catholic parishes from putting steeples atop their churches.

British Calvinists who fled to Frankfurt in 1554 during the reign of Mary Stuart, Queen of the Scots, apparently fared much better in their reception by the predominantly Lutheran community. When the exiles, headed by Scottish reformer John Knox returned to England five years after the execution of that tragic queen, they presented the city with a silver chalice in the form of a column crowned by a figure of victory. Known as the "English Monument", the 400-year-old relic, elaborately decorated and looking as new as the day it was presented, is on view to this day in the city historical museum.

The 'English Monument' presented by Calvinists to the city of Frankfurt, 1559.

French Huguenots and Italians joined Frankfurt's mercantile elite in the succeeding centuries, living by the trade fair and in return contributing with their products, erudition and polished living style to the ever-increasing importance of Frankfurt as a trading center.

City authorities were able to steer a middle course through the bitter factional struggles of the Thirty Years' War, and brought Frankfurt out of it nearly unharmed while most of the neighboring towns were sacked and pillaged time and again by contending groups of hostile armies. But the composition of the fair shifted. The war had destroyed Germany's textile industry and made the country dependent on imported Dutch and English cloth, now on sale at the fairs in unprecedented quantities.

New demands for luxury goods also developed after the war, and stands bulged with oriental silks, spices, tropical fruits and precious essences for milady's dressing table. Italians contributed much to the city's growth during this period. The Bolongaro family, immigrants from Stresa on Lago Maggiore, made a fortune manufacturing snuff, and built a baroque palace in Hoechst on the outskirts of Frankfurt. Textile dealer Leonhardi became Frankfurt's richest merchant, and Georg von Guaita, son of a grocery proprietor rose by his skills in municipal politics to hold the office of Lord Mayor a record six terms between 1824 and 1838.

Trade dominated the face of the town until the emphasis shifted eastward to Leipzig, which had been holing fairs since the 15th century. Following the Napoleonic era, Leipzig took over Frankfurt's position as central Europe's first market. In keeping with the old traditions, the fairs in Frankfurt were re-instituted in this century and today are again considered among the leading markets of the western world.

Since the war, more than twenty million people have visited the fairgrounds for the semiannual display of the new products by exhibitors from around the world. Not only trade fairs but technical and highly specialized exhibits of the greatest variety have been put on view in Frankfurt since the first International Air Travel Show opened its doors from July to October 1909. Displayed then were balloons, aviator's gear and early prototypes of heavier-than-air aircraft. In the years since 1948 professional shows of butchers, bakers and candymakers have vied for honors with international automobile displays, fur and textile fairs, bicycle shows, household fairs and the radio, phonograph and television trade mart which has served to introduce hifi, stereo and color television to Germany and European audiences.

One of the most well-known of the many exhibitions in Frankfurt is the Book Fair, held every autumn, which brings to Frankfurt the representative output of publishers from Europe and overseas areas. Recent literary figures honored by the "Peace Prize of the German Book Trade" awarded annually at the book fair have included American author and playwright Thornton Wilder.

Generally, the Frankfurt fairs are technical exhibitions and thus are open only to bona fide purchasers. On the other hand, shows such as the International Motor Show are open to any and all interested individuals.

The trend at the Frankfurt Fair is toward specialization. Thus in many technical fields the Frankfurt Fair has developed the reputation of being the leading exhibition of that industry in the world.

While technical progress has brought a continuing change of content and emphasis to the Frankfurt fairs, their basic role as a bridge of commerce between nations has remained unchanged from the days when armed horsemen of the citizen's militia would ride out beyond the city walls to escort foreign merchants to the fairgrounds and bid them welcome with a goblet of wine and the proverbial pretzel.

The historic symbol of the free city.

THE GHETTO

Frankfurt's decimated Jewish community, one of the oldest and most sorely tried in western Europe, dates back to the time of Charlemagne. For eight hundred years it has fluctuated between opulence and intellectual attainment on the one hand and second-class citizenship, economic deprivation and brutal physical extermination during the Hitler period. Early records refer to privileges accorded to traveling Jews by Charlemagne and his son, Ludwig the Pious. With Frankfurt already a trading center it is probable that some of them stayed in the royal city to carry on trade with goods from the Orient brought up from Mediterranean trade routes by other members of their scattered group.

The Jewish community was first mentioned in the late 12th century and consisted of less than 30 families. During the 13th and 14th centuries, they were confined in narrow quarters without the rights of citizens. The community had grown to 2,400 in the early 18th century and to 30,000, or almost 6,3 percent of the city's total population, just before the Nazis started their terror regime. Less than one percent of this total, some 300 Jewish returnees, came back to Frankfurt after the war; their number has now increased to about 4,000. Those who escaped death in the concentration camps of this century are today scattered in all directions. Only the 150,000 graves in the city's three Jewish cemeteries, from the simple asymmetric markers of the 13th century to the elaborate marble mausoleums of the

Rothschilds erected in the 19th century, bear mute witness to a once-thriving community. Its first spiritual leader was Rabbi Simon Hadarshan, who lived around 1220, according to Judaica in the Rothschild collection, now owned by the municipal library.

Old-line Frankfurters are the first to admit that the city today is poorer intellectually and artistically for the near-loss of its Jewish community. They provided much of the spirit of the metropolis, the sophistication, elegance and financial importance that made Frankfurt known around the globe. The arts flourished under their patronage, bons mots were coined daily and a truly patrician spirit prevailed among Frankfurt's great mercantile family clans of all religious persuasions who had 'more wine in their cellars than water in their wells', in the words of an old local saying.

Frankfurt's municipal mailmen in the 15th century (sketch by anonymous city clerk in tax ledger)

Forced by law and custom during the Middle Ages into restrictive occupations like pawnbrokerage, peddling and money lending, the Jewish community, concentrated in its separate ghetto as wards of the Empire, became the target of popular attack whenever economic conditions provided the incentive to look for scapegoats. In 1241 and 1349 they were driven from the city and their property confiscated in a series of popular outbreaks against the high interest rate legally stipulated for loans of all kinds. Reflecting uncertain economic conditions and the general insecurity of life in an age of armed scuffles, pestilence and servitude, the interest rate ran up to 43 % a year. It frequently led to the forced sale of debtors' personal possessions, moves that released the pent-up hatred of low income groups who found themselves constantly in bad debt. But to the royal court, the landed nobility and the patricians of the town, the presence of Jewish money-lenders was a convenience, for they provided a quick source of funds and credits to finance festivities, war expenditures and construction in a day and age that considered the pursuits of work or trade beneath the dignity of the landed aristocracy. For this reason, Jews were placed under the protection of the crown as serfs of the imperial household, with responsibility for their lives and property delegated to the city council. In return for an annual cash payment, the council issued a fixed number of residence permits which did not carry any of the rights or privileges of citizenship in the Imperial City of Frankfurt.

Several times, when the indebtedness of the nobility and clergy reached threatening proportions, the emperor was prevailed upon to issue an edict cancelling all previous obligations. Excesses, in the course of which the ghetto was sacked and looted by aroused mobs, were permitted or even inspired and the Jews conveniently driven from the city, leaving behind them loans they could not collect.

Living under these uncertain conditions, ghetto dwellers sought by the same token to hedge against the probability of expulsion, plunderings and capital losses by charging usurious interest rates that would allow a quick profit. It was a vicious circle.

Before the onset of the 19th century, two more major catastrophes decimated Frankfurt's Jewish population. In 1614 the artisans' guilds of Frankfurt, led by candymaker Vincenz Fettmilch seized the city in a revolutionary move against the corrupt city council, a group they claimed with much justice to be run by and for the patricians. Enraged journeymen, informed by imperial emissaries of likely consequences of their continued flouting of government authority, gave vent to their feelings by plundering the ghetto in a day-long pitched battle with its outnumbered defenders. A massacre was prevented when Fettmilch, the leader of the rebellion—he was later beheaded for sedition—allowed the Jewish population free passage out of the city. Contemporary records put the personal property loss of the Jewish community in the guild revolt of 1614 at an equivalent of 170,000 dollars. Less than a hundred years later in 1711, the entire ghetto was destroyed by fire, and other holocausts in 1719 and 1721 hampered reconstruction efforts, besides destroying the little left over from the earlier fire. The 1719 conflagration laid much of Frankfurt in ashes, it was known as 'The Great Gentiles' Fire' (der große Christenbrand) to distinguish it from 'The Great Jews' Fire' (der große Judenbrand) of 1711. Bad luck comes in bunches. During the same period, Frankfurt's Jewish community suffered financial setbacks in the general depression that followed the mercantile speculation failures of John Law, the ingenious Englishman whose wild colonisation schemes were backed by powerful money interests.

Trading enterprises that had received large credits before Law's financial empire tumbled went bankrupt, and the community, already badly hit by natural catastrophes, had to turn for help in the crisis to Emperor Charles VI. The sovereign forthwith ordered the city council to protect Jews from pressing creditors and support them in their efforts to collect outstanding debts "in order that they may once again be in a position to serve the public".

The relative isolation of the ghetto and the occupational restrictions in force for its occupants continued until Frankfurt became a Grand Duchy. The first and only Grand Duke, Napoleon's protégé Carl von Dalberg, Archbishop of Mainz and Prince Primate of the short-lived Rhine Federation, gave his domain a new constitution which granted all inhabitants equality before the law and equal political and economic opportunities. Under the terms of the constitution, Frankfurt's Jews obtained full equality of treatment and all civil rights, including the opportunity to apply for the costly and jealously-guarded privilege of citizenship. A citizen of Frankfurt traditionally occupied a status paralleling that of the nobility by being responsible directly to imperial authority instead of owing allegiance to any of the kingdoms and principalities that together made up the loose federation of the 'Holy Roman Empire'. For the duration of Dalberg's duchy from 1810—1814 and again after 1866 when the city was annexed by Prussia, Frankfurt lost its independent, practically sovereign status.

Though motivated largely by the new concepts of human dignity and emancipation sweeping Europe after the French revolution, von Dalberg was not averse to the thought of obtaining revenue for the duchy's coffers in decreeing civil rights for Frankfurt's Jewry. With a one-time payment equalling half a million dollars, 645 heads of Jewish households inscribed themselves and their families into the Frankfurt citizens' register in January 1812.

Looking back at the position of the ghetto community in 1792 from the enlightened vantage point of 1834, local historian Philip Jacob Doering wrote in his 'New Chronicle':

"Even though they were no longer persecuted and mistreated, the Jews continued to face pressure from outside, confined as they were in their narrow, evil-smelling street. At night and on Sundays they were not permitted outside their ghetto street, nor could they shop in the city's market before 10 a. m. to give first choice to their more fortunate contemporaries. Specified squares and districts, like the Roemerberg and cathedral hill, were off limits to them at all times, their occupation limited to peddling and money-lending. Educational opportunities were few, their place of worship resembled a storage vault more than a house of God, their garments were soiled and ill-fitting, and the dank air of their narrow street blighted them with pitiful disease. Many had the scabies, and all of them looked pale and sickly, for sunlight never penetrated the twisted warrens of the ghetto. To have them recognized instantly, Jews were forced to wear long black cloaks and prohibited from carrying canes, to say nothing of weapons.

"The Jews of that period, in short, provided a sad picture of downtrodden humanity. The intolerance and indifference with which they were treated went counter to the teachings of Jesus, and yet it was demanded of them that they ought to become Christians. But how could the traditional adversaries of Christendom be asked to consider as Christians their fellow men who had adopted as a way of life intolerance, injustice, indifference and persecution?"

The gradual emancipation of Frankfurt's Jewish community throughout the late 18th and early 19th century coincided with the rise of the Rothschild banking family in Europe. Meyer Amschel Rothschild and his five sons had introduced the modern system of trading in securities, had financed several royal governments and placed in Europe's financial centers obligations incredibly equivalent to more than one billion dollars. This at a time when the total annual budget of the United States amounted to 18 million dollars. With each of his five sons located in one of Europe's major financial centers, Meyer Amschel Rothschild of Frankfurt, who started his career in a ghetto exchange booth converting foreign monies during the annual trade fairs, obtained near control of the finances of the continent inside a generation. While he parlayed into a huge fortune the funds entrusted into his care with liberal profit-sharing provisions by the Prince of Hesse, his son Nathan, who lived in London, profited by running British goods to the continent during Napoleon's blockade.

Amschel Meyer, his oldest son, devoted himself to increasing the family fortunes from the banking headquarters established at Frankfurt.

Together with James in Paris, Salomon in Vienna, and Carl Mayer in Naples, he undertook daring speculations that managed to turn to the family's financial advantage every set of prevailing political circumstances.

Determined skill, daring and, importantly, luck were the components of the fabulous Rothschild success. Soon the brothers were indispensable to government operations, kings courted their favor, and the Austrian Emperor conferred upon them status of barons in the hereditary nobility. Frankfurt's Rothschilds, and with them the Jews

Tle tombstones of the Rothschild family in Frankfurt's Jewish cemetery on Rat Beil Strasse.

of Europe, had arrived. They had become 'salonfähig',—
the quality of being fit to appear in the drawing rooms
of the aristocracy.

Meyer Amschel, a rotund man in a grey cutaway who
posted himself daily on his private straw mat in the
Frankfurt Stock Exchange, buying, selling, issuing securities was in a true sense, a world power. His frowns, his
gestures, his changing expressions were considered a baro-
meter of international finance. His posture dictated the
exchange rate. One of Germany's greatest poets, Heinrich
Heine, himself of Jewish descent, wrote in those days:
"Money is the God of our age and Rothschild is his
prophet." But there was another side to the Rothschild
character.

Hans Christian Andersen told the story of Frau Rothschild's loyalty to her old home in the form of a fairy tale
typical of his style:

"It was in Frankfurt. I saw a strange scene there, the
moon said. My rays fell on a stately house. It was not the
house in which Goethe was born, nor the old city hall
with its barred windows behind which bleached the skulls
of the oxen roasted on spits at each emperor's coronation.
It was the house of a commoner, painted green and it
stood near the narrow streets of the Jewish quarter. It
was Rothschild's house.

"I looked through the open door. The staircase was lit
brightly. Servants stood along the stairs holding heavy
silver candelabra. They bowed deeply before a wrinkled
old lady who was carefully carried downstairs in a gilt
sedan chair. The head of the household stood at the landing. He kissed the old lady's hand respectfully. It was his

mother. She nodded gently to him and to the servants who escorted her down a gloomy lane to the plain door of a weatherbeaten cottage. She lived here. Here she had raised her sons and here she had known the fortune that had smiled on her family. If she would scorn all this, the ill-reputed street, the simple old home, fortune too would forsake her; that was her firm belief. The moon finished his tale. Tonight he had paid me but a short visit. But my thoughts lingered for long with the old woman in the dark narrow street. Only a word from her, and a glittering palace would spring upon the Thames, but a nod and a magnificent villa would be her own on the Gulf of Naples.

"If I leave this lowly small house in which the fortune of my sons had its beginning, the stars of their success would surely set. This was the belief that governed her actions. A superstition? Perhaps. But superstition of a special kind. And if you know the tale and have before your eyes the picture painted by the moon, two words suffice to spell its meaning: A mother."

The challenge of competition on an equal footing with the astute merchants and financiers relieved of their ghetto restrictions, not only served to quicken the pace of Frankfurt's commercial life, it also helped to develop a liberal and cosmopolitan atmosphere in which the arts and sciences represented by outstanding men of all religious persuasions flourished increasingly. Among the Christians and Jews who worked together in Frankfurt during the 19th century were the philosopher Arthur Schopenhauer, the revolutionary author Ludwig Boerne, Moritz von Bethmann the banker, Felix Mendelssohn-Bartholdy the

Memorial tablet affixed to the Frankfurt residence of Anne Frank, 1957.

('In this house lived Anne Frank, born 12/6/1929 at Frankfurt on the Main She died as a victim of National-Socialist persecution in the Bergen-Belsen concentration camp, 1945. Her life and death is our obligation

The youth of Frankfurt')

composer, Dr. Heinrich Hoffmann creator of world-famous children's books like 'Struwwelpeter', Professor Paul Ehrlich, the discoverer of the drug that freed mankind from the curse of syphilis, Rudolf Christian Boettger, inventor of gun cotton and the safety match, and the liberal publisher Leopold Sonnemann whose *Frankfurter Zeitung* enjoyed world-wide repute.

The spirit of enlightenment characterized in Frankfurt by a strong sense of civic responsibility in all quarters of the population continued far into the 20th century, until the Nazi terror put the clock back to the dark ages. But enough memories of liberal traditions remained to make Hitler detest the city that had once been the cradle of German democracy. He set foot inside Frankfurt only twice, and it was a 14 year old Frankfurt girl named Anne Frank who scribbled into her diary on a back street of Amsterdam one of the century's most moving human documents. She was born in the city, she died in the Belsen concentration camp. Her simple words summed up man's inhumanity to man in a way that stopped the heart-beat of a generation. Present-day Frankfurt perpetuates her memory in the name of a school and a commemorative plaque at her birthplace at Ganghofer Strasse 24.

Seal of a Frankfurt-Mayor 1245.

"The five Frankfurters", the five sons of Mayer Amschel Rothschild, born in
Frankfurt and given nobility status by the Emperor of Austria in 1822.
Above: Amschel Mayer in Frankfurt. Left: Nathan Mayer in London. Right:
Salomon Mayer in Wien. Below: Carl Mayer in Neapel and James Mayer in
Paris.

The ancestral home of the Rothschilds in the Jewish quarter of the old city, built 1711 and destroyed during the war in 1944. Mayer Amschel Rothschild, the founder of the Frankfurt banking dynasty lived there until his death in 1812. (Early photograph by C. F. Mylius.)

Interior of Frankfurt's synagogue on Freiherr vom Stein Strasse. Restored in 1950. The mosaics were created by Hans Leistikow.

Motif from the old Jewish cemetery at Frankfurt. Tombstone from 1773.

Carl Theodor von Dalberg (1744-1817). Grand Duke of Frankfurt from 1806 to 1813.

THE GRAND DUCHY

In a sense it is a paradox of history that the French Revolution, conceived to end the power of the nobility and the clergy, started a chain of circumstances by which Frankfurt, a kind of city republic run by protestant commoners, was turned into a Grand Duchy, ruled by an Archbishop. Five times French troops occupied Frankfurt, first during the Seven-years-war (Count Thoranc in Goethe's native house!), again as revolutionary forces under General Custine in 1792, again in 1796, under Jourdan in 1800 and finally in 1806, this time as Napoleon's forces commanded by General Augereau.

Five years before, Napoleon, whose star had risen quickly, forced Francis, last of the Roman Emperors, to cede to France all lands left of the Rhine. City fathers, who had sought to steer a neutral course through the Napoleonic wars, dutifully accepted the French occupation, even sending emissaries to Napoleon's coronation and dipping deep into municipal coffers and the pockets of the moneyed classes to pay provisioning contributions demanded by the occupation forces. This included four million gold francs levied by Jourdan and the same amount paid to Augereau. But the protection monies obligingly assembled and eagerly accepted were all in vain. In 1806, Napoleon turned over the city as a present to Carl von Dalberg, Archbishop of Mainz, as a reward for the latter's loyalty to the French cause. Dalberg, one of the three ecclesiastical electors of the realm had served as a tool of Napoleon's policies in accepting the nominal leadership of the French protectorates left of the Rhine. His title was 'Prince Primate of the Rhine Confederation.'

The Primate made Frankfurt the capital of his domain four weeks after Emperor Francis, acknowledging the fact that the Holy Roman Empire had ceased to exist in name as well as in fact, renounced the meaningless title in favor of a more accurate 'Emperor of Austria.'

The paintings of the Holy Roman Emperors in the Kaisersaal of the Roemer were discreetly covered with red cloth as the city council swore allegiance to France before a French commissioner to shouts of 'Long live the Emperor Napoleon' sent up from the square below by occupation troops and supporters of the new regime. The date: September 9, 1806.

Frankfurt became known as 'the sovereign territory of the Prince Primate', his initial C was placed in gold on the Eschenheimer tower, now renamed 'Carlstor' and an extensive program of municipal reform was started in the name of the ambitious prince of the church. With the tearing-down of the old fortifications and the leveling of the moats, the city lost its medieval character, and new tax legislation, accompanied by police and social reforms of unquestionable merit, counterbalanced the pressures of inflation and censorship.

In 1810 Napoleon, then at the height of his power, conferred on Dalberg the title of 'Grand Duke of Frankfurt'. Eugene Beauharnais, Napoleon's stepson, was named as his heir-apparent. The Grand Duchy, closely integrated with France, measured about 100 square miles, had some 300,000 inhabitants and included besides the city of

Frankfurt, the area from Mainz to Aschaffenburg, the bishopric of Fulda, the county of Hanau and the city of Wetzlar. Napoleon visited his dependency several times during the victorious campaigns against the combined Austro-Prussian forces. Triumphal arches to commemorate Napoleon's victories lined the Zeil, today Frankfurt's broad avenue of department stores. Some carried modest slogans like 'Immortalité, Prudence, Victoire' next to the names of places made famous by Napoleon's victories—'Tilsit, Austerlitz, Friedland'.

When Josephine followed him to Frankfurt, a grand ball was given in honor of the imperial couple in the municipal theatre, but the cheers for the illustrious Corsican from the throats of local supporters who had obtained economic and social advantages in the changeover, turned to curses when the continental blockade began to interfere with trade and Frankfurt's young men were drafted to fight for Napoleon's cause in far-away Spain and Russia. The confiscation and destruction of British goods, mainly textiles, in a bonfire outside the city caused widespread indignation. Coupled with the prohibitive tariff on colonial goods, French economic warfare moves directed against the commerce vital to Frankfurt did much to shake von Dalberg's position. He became the symbol of popular hatred directed against Napoleon, even though he interceded with the Emperor on numerous occasions in Frankfurt's behalf.

Grand Duke von Dalberg, well-intentioned but impractical, was a social reformer concerned with projects beyond his time, among them the establishment of a university in Frankfurt and the construction of a dirigible called Dalberg's 'air fish'. Completely tied to the political fortunes of Napoleon who installed him in office, he was not to enjoy for long the title and privileges of a sovereign. Along with other supporters of Napoleon, the Grand Duke of Frankfurt abdicated and fled the city as the French armies retreated to the western bank of the Rhine after their crushing defeat at Leipzig in 1813. Von Dalberg retired to Regensburg, dying there as bishop in 1817.

Cloisters of the Carmelite Monastery with remnants of murals by Jörg Ratgeb, 1515.

THE GARDEN CITY

From a walled and turreted medieval city with moats in which stag were kept for the banquets of the city council, Frankfurt evolved to a suburban garden spot during the eighteenth and nineteenth centuries. Summer residences and villas of the wealthier citizens were scattered in private estates all along the approaches to the city. The old walls and fortifications were torn down, moats leveled and the newly-won real estate parcelled out as gardens among the city's patrician families. Downtown Frankfurt owes its green belt to the building regulations which permitted only pavilions on the newly-claimed land and made each owner set aside a portion of his property for use as a public park.

On the approaches of the city, now partly occupied by offices, factories and housing projects, every family that could afford it would build its stone and stucco summer residences along strict classical lines surrounded by flower beds, covered walks and vineyards. The back-to-nature movement—part of the romantic spirit of the age—expressed itself in gardening, in the inclusion of horticulture among the fine arts, in elaborate flower arrangements and in popular paintings of idyllic country scenes. Moneyed and titled citizens vied with each other in the elegance of their garden houses, the spaciousness of their private parks and the care lavished on them by their gardeners. A contemporary account tells of the elaborate garden party and fireworks display staged November 18, 1741 by the Spanish

Garden pavillon of the d'Orville family on the approaches to the city, circa 1740.

ambassador Count Montijo in the summer house of lawyer J. M. von Loën.

In honor of Queen Elizabeth's name day, the garden paths and the house were illuminated by 40,000 colored lanterns and the arcades leading to a 'hall of hundred mirrors' decorated with greenery. Five hundred invited society figures witnessed the impressive fireworks display. Goethe's parents incidentally were married in the same garden house in 1748; attorney von Loën was the poet's maternal great-uncle.

More than 500 garden houses were built on the city's outskirts during the eighteenth century. Their number increased when the city leveled its ramparts in 1806 under the administration of Mayor Jacob Guiollett in the days

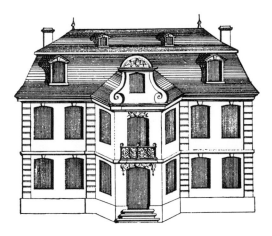

The garden house of the Gontards at the old windmill, near the present-day site of the Nizza gardens.

of the short-lived Grand Duchy. Guiollett, in a sense the creator of the garden city, opened the door to Frankfurt's continued growth. His monument, created more than a century ago stands in the Taunus Anlage. Today this section of Frankfurt's front yard, created by Guiollett, faces Germany's 'banking row', main offices of the nation's major financial establishments, in which gold bullion once again is being traded over the counter as in the 'golden age' before World War I.

The external appearance of an 18th century Frankfurt garden house has been preserved in today's downtown area by the single-story structure in the park behind the opera house ruin, used in the summer months for exhibits of the city's art galleries.

Collector and art patron Johann Christian Gerning commissioned a master engraver to provide detailed drawings of the rococo and late baroque pavilions on the city's garden outskirts. It is to Heinrich Wicker, the engraver who lived in the mid-eighteenth century that we owe the likenesses of the buildings that played so large a part in the city's social life. Hardly a trace remains of them in present-day Frankfurt. Some of the garden houses looked more like palaces with their sweeping stairways, elaborate stucco work, turreted roofs and bay windows. But in general they conformed to the classic line of the French country home in miniature and were used as such by their owners who fancied themselves in the role of country squires.

Prominent examples were the garden houses of Dr. Gottfried Mueller along the Sachsenhausen bank of the Main river, the house of the wealthy grocery merchant and later mayor, Guaita, with its broadside facade of ten windows jutting out at a right angle to the river shore near the Frankfurt side of today's Friedensbruecke (bridge of peace), and mayor Wiesenhuetten's summer house a few steps further down along the river bank. These summer residences not only presented a stately appearance from the outside, but were stocked with valuable furniture and paintings of the romantic school of which many were willed to the city's museums, where they remain preserved to this day.

The first sight greeting the visitor approaching the city with the weekly 'market ship' a hundred or more years ago was an uninterrupted row of well-tended gardens and stately summer homes that bore witness to the wealth and good taste of their owners. The closer one got to the city, the more lively the activity on both shores. Ships loading and unloading, and the bustle of trade in the crowded streets of the old city displayed to advantage the booming business of Frankfurt's merchant population.

Approaching the city by land as well, the traveler would find it embedded in garden surroundings. From afar could be seen the spire of the cathedral. Later he would pass by the country estates and gardens, the guard tower remnants of the medieval belt of outer fortifications, the leveled inner moats turned into lawns, orchards and flower beds. Only then would the traveler enter the inner city, in those days at most a tenth of its present size and population.

A notable departure from the classic garden pavilion was the Russian-style dacha, modeled on the Tsar's garden house at Tsarskoye Seloe near St. Petersburg (now

Memorial to Consul Bethmann's horse in Park Louisa, Sachsenhausen.

Leningrad), put up in 1810 south of the city by banker Simon Moritz von Bethmann, honorary consul of imperial Russia. Located on Moerfelder Landstraße, in back of the Louisa playground, the property consists of a bark-covered dacha surrounded by a spacious park, complete with pond, a teahouse and a bathhouse. A bronze statue of a horse, half life-size, stands atop a small mound inside the private park, perhaps the only memorial to a horse in Europe, certainly the only one in Frankfurt. The statue is the work of sculptor Christian Rauch commissioned in memory of Bethmann's favorite mare who saved her master's life by eluding pursuers during a skirmish in the Napoleonic wars. Tsar Alexander I of Russia stayed at Bethmann's country dacha, reminiscent of his own summer retreat, in 1814 on his way to the Congress of Vienna. It was the Alexander who had defeated Napoleon's armies, an impassioned mystic torn between social reform and the blackest reaction. His life long he was haunted by secret guilt for abetting the palace revolt that did away with Paul I, his benighted and tyrannical father. A number of historians state that Alexander did not die as is commonly supposed in 1824 but that he feigned his own death at Taganrog on the Black Sea and lived on as hermit Fyodor Kuzmich in Siberia until 1864.

Not far from Park Louisa stands the Sachsenhaeuser Warte, one of four lookout towers guarding the approaches to the city. Built in 1468, it has survived a half dozen wars, pestilence and holocausts like its brethren to the north, west and east of the city. Not so with the city's inner fortifications. Only the Eschenheimer tower, today a much-reproduced symbol of the city against the silhouette

Sachsenhaeuser Warte,
a remnant of the outer belt of medieval watch towers

of the telecommunications building, survived the razing of
the walls in the early 19th century. It was a Frenchman
who saved the tower from the modern improvement zeal
of the French-oriented city administration. The Comte de
Hedouville, Napoleon's ambassador to the short-lived
duchy created by his sovereign, personally intervened with
Grand Duke von Dalberg to save the fabled tower for
posterity.

Built in its present shape in 1426, on the site of an
older tower dating back to 1346, the place is rife with
local legends. Among them the prophesy that the tower
will remain standing as a proud symbol of bygone days
until the ivy covering its lower portion has climbed all
the way up to engulf the weather vane. Judging by the
rate the ivy is growing, it seems safe to say that Frankfurt
will enjoy the tower for some years to come.

Eschenheimer Tower

The weather vane too has its story. Poaching was capital offense in the Middle Ages and when Hans Winkelsee, the notorious poacher of the city's forest preserves was finally caught, he was locked up in tower's garret chamber just below the weather vane, pending his execution. For nine days and nights the creaking of the rusty vane just above robbed him of sleep and he resolved that as a last wish he would ask to shoot the figure nine into the tin flag, hoping that the city council would be so impressed with his feat as to give him his freedom. He made this request to the jailer and the council agreed to his release should he perform the seemingly impossible trick. You guessed it. There was a jailer's daughter who fell in love with the handsome prisoner. She climbed up on the roof the night before the test, and secured the vane in place with a wooden wedge so as to present a steady target. Of course, Winkelsee made good his offer, was set free, married the daughter and obtained an appointment as chief forester. They lived happily ever after. Next time you go past the Eschenheimer tower glance up at the weather vane. The crowd that will begin to gather has probably never heard this story.

The razing of the old town walls created a great stir in Germany and beyond. Goethe's mother wrote: "The old ramparts have been leveled and the old gates pulled down. The stuffy powdered wigs hereabouts would have never been capable of this innovation." And Alexandre Dumas, taking a vacation from the 'Three Musketeers' and his other prodigious writings, had this to say of Frankfurt on his trip through the Rhineland in 1838: "Instead of old walls and stagnant moats, the citizens of Frankfurt have created a charming English garden, an elegant fragrant belt of green which permits a walk around the city in the shade of magnificent trees along neat gravel paths. With its white, green and pink houses Frankfurt appears as a bouquet of camelias in a wreath of heather. The grave stone of the mayor who thought out this improvement rises amidst the garden labyrinth, peopled every day at five o'clock in the afternoon by the citizens and their families."

Private and public parks in the city's outskirts at the time of Dumas' visit today are located in the heart of the downtown area but the expansion of the park and playground area has kept pace with the city's growth. Young Goethe searched for easter eggs in the family orchard, in an area where today soldiers 'police-up' behind the Abrams (previously I. G. Farben) building, and the Rothschilds held court, two generations later, at the palace they built in adjoining Grueneburg Park.

The private estates of other noble families like Holzhausen, Brentano and Count Solms also located on Frankfurt's approaches, were gradually acquired for public use by the city, and today comprise an essential part of the 2,500 acres of public parks and playgrounds, currently available to the city's population. Outside the city limits, the municipal forest, some 10,000 acres of it, stretches ten miles beyond Rhein-Main airport, halfway to Darmstadt.

Interspersed with the city's parks and the forest recreation areas are some 400 children's playgrounds for the more than 100,000 kids of the city. Many of these playgrounds are equipped with unconventional games, merry-go-rounds, swings and climbing apparatus.

Some of the parks are set aside specially for treading on the lawns; no 'keep off' sign mars the recreation area and visitors are encouraged to cavort on the lawns and to use them for picnic purposes. Two of these unusual parks are located in the east of the city, the Huth and Ost Park.

Tall old trees in the downtown area are the pride of the municipal parks authority. Oaks and yews, more than 300 years old, are grouped together in the botanical gardens and a plane tree, 70 feet tall and 170 years old spreads its branches near the Eschenheimer Tower. At the other end of Eschersheimer Landstrasse, near the suburb of that name, stands the famous Eschenheimer Linden, which was planted in 1648 at the conclusion of the '30 years war', and thus is sometimes referred to as the "Peace Linden". In recent years the ravages of time have begun to take their toll, and the services of a tree surgeon to the extent of over

Three hundred year old linden tree along Eschersheimer Landstrasse.

4,000 dollars were required to save the historical old tree. At latest count, some 24,000 trees line Frankfurt's streets, and each year nature-conscious city fathers celebrate the 'Day of the Tree', planting a seedling in memory of a great citizen. But, even though nearly 5,000 new trees are planted every year along the streets of Frankfurt, the total number of trees remains approximately constant, due to the loss of trees from old age, disease and as victims of widening streets.

Ten minutes by car from the heart of the city lies Frankfurt's Waldstadion, the sports arena embedded in the forest, which includes a football field, several race courses and complete facilities for track and field championships. The 300 foot swimming pool adjoining the sports arena has been the site of German national swimming events. The first Workers' Olympic Games brought half a million people to the Frankfurt arena in 1925 as the initial international sports event in the interwar period. Following its recent reconstruction and enlargement, the stadium has a capacity for 62,000 spectators, and is used for sports contests of national and international significance. Underlining the town's importance as a sports center is the move to Frankfurt of organizations like the German Olympic Society, the national association of sports clubs, and the Federal Sports School, where Germany's Olympic hopefuls train.

Characteristic of local sports activities are the varied horse races at the Niederrad course and the rowing regattas held on the Main river practically every weekend during the summer seasons. Onlookers gather in the Nizza Gardens to watch the progress of their favorite boating clubs from riverside benches nestling among the flowers and bushes of the colorful promenade. Laid out by the city a century ago in place of the winter harbor fallen into disuse, the semi-tropical plants and elaborate flower arrangements of the garden gave rise to its popular name, the German version of the beauty spot Nice on the French Riviera. But the similarity ends with the flowers. You have probably noted that it doesn't extend to the weather.

Spring comes later to Frankfurt than to Nice and in winter the Main river sometimes shows a nasty tendency to freeze over, something the Mediterranean can hardly be accused of. Even in Goethe's time, Frankfurt citizens amused themselves ice skating on the frozen river, and the poet has left us a description of how as a child he borrowed his mother's red sable-trimmed coat as he went figure-skating with his cronies in the cold winter of 1773. At that time, and again in 1784, a thick layer of ice covered the river all through January and February. The Sachsen-hausen shore could be reached by a horse-drawn coach and on foot without bothering to use the bridge, and a con-temporary sketch by Zehender shows local youths and a few dignified burghers amusing themselves on the ice against the backdrop of the city's characteristic silhouette. The Main froze over as recently as the bitter cold winter of 1956, when similar scenes were re-enacted, though the more cautious Frankfurters of the mid-twen-tieth century did not venture as far from the shore as had their horse-drawn forebears two centuries ago.

Whenever the Main froze over, the coopers' guild staged a contest on the ice, climaxed by the making of a large barrel and the joint consumption of the contents of numerous smaller barrels, accompanied by the blare of the guild's brass music.

But the river was not always a passively cooperative partner in the fun and commerce of succeeding generations; occasionally the waters of the Main reared up and reminded the Frankfurters of their power over the works of man. Terse notes by city chroniclers over the centuries show an unexpected side of the peaceful Main: "1342—the river was so high that it tore off a portion of the Stone Bridge and water stood two feet deep in St. Bartholomew's. Bernhard Rohrbach and Johann Brum rowed a boat into the Carmelite Monastery when the waters of the Main washed up the city hall steps in 1354." Again in 1540 the river reached up to the fountain on Roemerberg square and in 1633, goods stored in Roemerberg vaults for the Frankfurt fair were spoiled by the flood. Debris, smashed boats, and the carcasses of animals (including a

The cathedral amidst Frankfurt's old parks and new buildings.

coach with its team of four horses dead in the traces), were seen floating past the old bridge.

In the nineteenth century, the grading of the river bank and the construction of locks upstream made the floods a thing of the past. Most of the building along the river have been torn down and rebuilt a number of times in the course of the centuries. But today as before the cathedral dominates the old city skyline, and enough other landmarks have been reconstructed in their original form, permitting here and there a fleeting glimpse of the city through the ages. But even though the city has changed, the human substance has remained. And the waters of the Main, which centuries ago silently witnessed tokens changing hands to gain admission past the medieval city gate, today silently witness tokens changing hands to gain admission for Frankfurt's motorized population to the drive-in theaters on the city's approaches.

Token used to gain admission past the city gates after hours. This early nineteenth century specimen admits cart drawn by two horses.

Revolutionaries and Conservatives

Of all German cities, Frankfurt felt the breath of freedom first, and it felt it the strongest. The seat of the
central authority of the German Federation, created
by the Congress of Vienna, replacing the Holy Roman
Empire, Frankfurt played host in its walls to the diplomatic maneuverings of representatives from the 38 sovereign German states that emerged out of Napoleon's wars.
The object of this 'Bundestag' was ostensibly to guarantee
peace within the federation and the independence of its
member states. But the emissaries of the princes were concerned mainly with upholding their sovereigns' rights to
rule as autocrats over the various parts of the country.

For dynastic reasons the assembly opposed the creation
of a strong central authority and the participation in
government of representatives elected directly by the
people. Legislative processes in the Bundestag turned
mainly into a jockeying for position by the smaller monarchies, dukedoms and principalities in the developing
struggle for leadership of the German Federation between
the Austrian Empire and the Kingdom of Prussia.

This enraged the liberals and student groups, astir
with the ideals of nationalism and the unity of German-
speaking countries. They had fought the wars against
Napoleon to free Germany from foreign rule and considered a return to the petty bickerings among princes
ruling 'by divine right' without the consent of the governed a betrayal of their fondest aspirations.

Austria's chancellor, Prince Metternich, and Prussia's Otto von Bismarck, in those days himself a delegate to the Bundestag, were in the forefront of repressive measures against the liberal movement.

In April 1833, a group of desperate student leaders attempted to overpower the guard posts, seize the arsenals in Frankfurt and overthrow the federal assembly by force of arms, in order to proclaim a single Germany under a central government. They stormed the Hauptwache and the Konstablerwache, then the main guard posts of the local garrison, and took the defenders by surprise. But the leaders of the revolt were soon overwhelmed and imprisoned by military reinforcements hurriedly called to the scene of the action.

The organizers of the revolt all came from Frankfurt, and most of them managed to escape, making their way to the United States, where they distinguished themselves in later life in state and federal government positions. Some of them even rose to top-ranking positions in the Union armies during the Civil War.

Years of oppressions of liberal thought followed. In 1848 the seizure of Paris by the Commune inspired a new generation of students and liberals in central Europe to rise up against their absolute monarchs. The initial and widespread success of the revolt caught the established governments by surprise and rulers everywhere were forced to yield or stall for time by promising a broad range of political and social reforms.

A provisional assembly of liberals met in Frankfurt, calling for universal and secret balloting to choose a German constitutional assembly. Two months later, the in-

Church of St. Paul

tellectual elite of Germany, more than 800 representatives from all member states of the federation, assembled in Frankfurt. They met at the Kaisersaal of the Roemer, previously the site of imperial pageantry, and moved from there in solemn procession amidst the ringing of church bells and the firing of salutes by the citizens' militia to the church of St. Paul, selected as their meeting place. The church—secularized for more than a century—has been known ever since as the 'cradle of German democracy.'

At the same time an 'Address of Sympathy' calling upon 'our German brothers' to become a single nation of free men, 'conceived in the spirit of Washington,' arrived from New York, signed by 500 Americans of German descent, many of them Frankfurters and including some who had participated in the ill-fated student revolt fifteen years earlier. Symbolically the appeal was dispatched to Germany on the *SS* Washington.

The Paul's Church Assembly met with the noblest of intentions. But as it brought together 800 high-minded intellectuals, most of them lawyers and professors, it quickly turned into an academic assembly discussing definitions fiercely, and airing at great length such topics as the rights of man. Clauses of the proposed constitution were drawn up laboriously, one by one, over a period of nearly a year. While the great debate proceeded, valuable time was lost and the sovereigns who might have acquiesced in the assembly's decisions while the revolutionary momentum was still carrying forward, had a chance to rally their forces.

In its initial moves however, the Paul's Church Assembly acted decisively. It dissolved the Bundestag and created instead a provisional government for all Germany, vesting supreme authority in Archduke Johann of Austria who was appointed imperial regent and chief of the provisional executive.

The Archduke, younger brother of Francis II, last of the Holy Roman Emperors, was 66 years old when called upon to serve as the 'people's choice' for the highest office of the nascent commonwealth. His popularity was due in no small part to the fact that he married a commoner and was a thorn in the side of the conservatives wielding decisive influence at the court in Vienna. With the election of Archduke Johann as the head of the provisional executive power—he was called 'the elected administrator of the empire', Frankfurt had become the capital of the first central government of Germany.

While the Frankfurt assembly was deliberately designing a constitution, incorporating features of the British and American systems, Archduke Johann confined himself to representational duties in a small palace put at his disposal on the corner of Eschenheimer and Stiftstrasse. Built by a banker named Muehlens, in 1802, the palace formerly was the Frankfurt residence of Prince Primate Carl von Dalberg, the one and only Grand Duke of Frankfurt. It was destroyed in 1944.

It took nearly a year, until March 1849, to complete the Paul's Church constitution which called for a federal state under a hereditary 'Emperor of the Germans' with a bicameral parliament chosen in national elections charged with the legislative, and a cabinet responsible to parliament, with the executive function of government. This blueprint for a constitutional monarchy included guarantees of civil liberties and equality under the law. Even before the constitution was adopted, however, trouble developed with Austria over the territory to be included in the projected German national state.

Under instructions from Vienna, representatives of the Habsburg monarchy declared that the multi-national Austrian Empire would join the projected federation as a single unit or not at all, but the majority in the Frankfurt parliament were opposed to the inclusion of non-German nationalities such as the Slavs, Hungarians and Italians in Habsburg territories, among the planned German national state. When Austria declined to join the commonwealth with its German-speaking territories only, as proposed by the high-minded but impractical assemblymen of St. Paul's, the crown of a German national state, excluding Austria, was offered to Frederick William IV, King of Prussia.

By that time the position of the monarchies had solidi-
fied in the face of parliamentary bickerings to the point
where once again, dynastic interests could be put foremost
in dealing with the impotent Frankfurt assembly. Frederick refused pointblank to accept a crown at the hands of
a popularly-elected assembly which had the temerity to
strike 'by the grace of God' from the royal title. Shortly
before the Prussian action, followed by the withdrawal
of Austria's representatives from the assembly, Frankfurt
saw street fighting when demagogues of the radical left
accused parliament of betraying to a Danish minority
the German population of Schleswig and Holstein in
concluding an armistice to stop an outbreak of fighting
between Prussia and Denmark. The war had started over
the minority issue on a pretext of disagreement over the
line of succession to the dukedoms.

Protest demonstrations ensued, and troops had to be
called out by the Frankfurt city government to protect
the national assembly. Enraged mobs attempted to storm
Paul's Church and failing that, barricaded themselves
in the old city from where they could be dislodged only
by artillery reinforcements brought up hurriedly from
Mainz and Darmstadt. Order was restored by the military late in the day, but 62 soldiers and 33 civilians
were killed in the street fighting. The reputation of the
national assembly as a champion of German unity had
suffered a fatal blow, betrayed by the rabble-rousing of
radical politicians.

Institution of the so-called 'mixed patrol' organized
to prevent a recurrence of bloodshed provided visible
proof of the assembly's failings to promote German

Procession of the delegates into Paul's Church on 18 May 1848.

The Assembly of Princes at the Thurn and Taxis palace in 1863. The meeting, called and chaired by Emperor Francis Joseph of Austria, was a last effort

to bring about a federal German state under the dynastic leadership of the Habsburgs.

ADRESSE
der
DEUTSCHEN BRÜDER
in dem freien
Staatenbunde Amerika's
an das
DEUTSCHE VOLK

New-York im April 1848.

Dem freien deutschen Volke!

Den vorbereitenden großen Bewegungen in Deutschland für eine endliche politische Wiedergeburt des Vaterlandes waren wir längst mit freudigem Interesse gefolgt; die Kunde von den Ereignissen, die als unmittelbare Folgen der Pariser Revolution in den süddeutschen Staaten zum Ausbruch kamen und wie ein elektrischer Schlag alle Theile unseres Vaterlandes durchzuckten, hatten wir jubelnd vernommen; — aber noch hing unser Blick mit bangen Erwartungen an den finstern Wetterwolken, die sich um Preußens Hauptstadt unheilschwanger und drohend zusammen zogen. Diese Wetterwolken, die letzten Ereignisse haben sie zerrissen und jubelnd begrüßen wir die Sonne der Freiheit, die nach so manchen schmachvoller Prüfung unserm Volke entgegen leuchtet, verheißend eine bessere, glücklichere Zukunft. Kein Oesterreich, kein Preußen! Ein einiges Deutschland! Ein Fürst sprach's und es blieb leerer Schall. Ein Volk will es und es wird zur That! Ja, Ihr deutschen Brüder! werdet, seyd, bleibt ein Volk, ein freies Volk, und laßt als solches Euch die brüderliche Hand aus dem einigen, freien Staatenbunde Amerika's reichen, der groß und blühend, weil er frei, stark und mächtig, weil er einig ist. So schreitet denn auch Ihr fort auf der einmal siegreich betretenen Bahn, mit Kraft und Muth, und was Ihr Edles begonnen, Ihr werdet es vollenden! Nicht auf den Verheißungen Eurer Fürsten beruht unsere Zuversicht; nein, auf dem kräftig erwachten Freiheitssinn der Nation, auf der Macht der öffentlichen Meinung. Ehre den Männern, die den richtigen Augenblick erfaßt und es verstanden haben, nicht allein den schlummernden Freiheitssinn des Volkes zu wecken, sondern auch demselben eine feste und bekannte Richtung zu geben. Ehre Denen, deren freie Worte zur kühnen That entflammen! Heil aber, drei Mal Heil ihnen, die selbst auf Leben und Tod den heiligen Kampf um des Volkes unveräußerliches Recht bestanden und Denen, welchen der Todesengel den Lorbeer um die blutigen Schläfe wand. Diesen Zuruf bringt Euch unser „Washington" geschmückt mit den Flaggen des freien Deutschlands, und wenn schwarz-roth-gold stolz neben dem Sternenbanner unserer Republik weht, wenn es Washingtons Geist ist, der beide Flaggen umschwebt, dann wird es diesseits und jenseits des Oceans in den Herzen aller deutschen Brüder jubelnd wiedertönen: „Gott segne Deutschland!"

Das Comite: Hessenberg,   Dr. H. Luwewig,
Christ,   J. Kuhnhardt,
Dr. Gescheidt,   Dr. Henschell,
W. Löschigk,   F. J. Schlesinger.

'Address of Sympathy' dispatched by 494 prominent German-Americans to the revolutionary assembly in Frankfurt, 1848.

unity. Austrian, Bavarian and Prussian military police-
men patrolled the streets of the city in mixed detachments
to keep order among riotous troops from the north and
south of Germany and to look out for signs of civil unrest
that might once again threaten the National Assembly.

Frankfurt's local poet Friedrich Stoltze lampooned this
institution in his humorous dialect writings. Caricatures
of this early MP patrol on its daily rounds were a fixture
in a good many upper middle class homes of Frankfurt
before the turn of the century. In a sense Frankfurt's
mixed patrol might be called a forerunner of the four
power jeep patrol in postwar Vienna.

With Prussia's king refusing to head a federation that
would have infringed on his royal prerogatives, the
months of exasperating debate in the assembly ended in
complete failure. Austrian and Prussian representatives
left Frankfurt and the remaining rump parliament moved
to Stuttgart, only to be dispersed there by government
troops in a humiliating finale to the revolt that started
off with a great promise but was caught unprepared by
its initial sweeping success.

With the failure of the attempt to unite Germany
under a parliamentary system, the autocratic governments, once again solidly entrenched, returned to their
old practice of persecuting the liberals. Archduke Johann
whose personal disappointment at having been passed
over in the assembly's election of an 'Emperor of the
Germans' in favor of the Prussian king compounded his
professional regret at the failure of the provisional
government he headed, left Frankfurt in December 1849.
Before his departure he correctly turned over his pro-

The 'mixed patrol' of Austrian, Prussian, Bavarian and Frankfurt military police keep order in the occupied city.

visional central authority to the returning Bundestag—
nothing more than an appointed diplomatic congress in
permanent session. Archduke Johann then returned to
his estates in Styria living another ten years to the age
of 77.

The failure of the Frankfurt assembly, accompanied
by the restoration of absolute rule, brought hundreds of
the nation's intellectual leaders to join the earlier generation of German liberals in America. Normalcy returned
to central Europe, but under the surface, the struggle
continued. In particular the *Frankfurter Zeitung*, a daily
newspaper founded in 1856 by banker Leopold Sonnemann, provided the rallying point of liberal sentiment
and a vehicle of biting attacks on government methods.
Though it gave rise to a series of protests by emissaries

of autocratic regimes, among them Otto von Bismarck of Prussia, it deftly avoided prosecution under the rigorous laws passed by the diet to muzzle the liberal press.

The rivalry between Austria and Prussia for leadership of the German federation became even more pronounced in the internal diplomatic maneuverings of the Bundestag. An open break was precipitated in 1863 when Austria made its final bid for a constitutional reform under the aegis of the Habsburg monarchy by inviting all the sovereigns of the German confederation to Frankfurt for an 'assembly of princes'. Emperor Francis Joseph, then a youthful 33, himself presided at the meeting of the princes in the Thurn und Taxis palace, but the assembly, though accompanied by extraordinary pomp and splendor, was doomed to failure from the outset when Prussia's King William on the advice of his chancellor Bismarck declined to attend after serving formal notice that his kingdom was not about to accept an Austrian solution to the nationalities problem. Instead, the Prussian government seeking to unite the German-speaking principalities on its own terms made no secret of regarding the Austrian move as unwarranted interference in its private hunting reserve.

Extravagant social events, reminiscent of Frankfurt's role as the coronation city marked the princes' assembly whenever the 29 crowned heads, seated around the immense green baize-covered conference table, were not engaged in futile discussions on the future of the German-speaking states.

Today only the baroque doorway of the palace remains as a counterpart to the super-modern telecommunications building of the German Federal Post Office, completed in 1955.

Open warfare broke out between Prussia and Austria in 1866, and within six weeks the Prussian armies inflicted a crushing defeat on the Austrian forces in the battle of Koeniggraetz. The news of this battle came as a shock to a considerable number of German states who had sided with Austria against Prussia, among them Bavaria, Hanover and Wuerttemberg. The Free City of Frankfurt also had voted for Austria at the crucial Bundestag meeting at which federal sanctions were imposed against Prussia for illegal intervention in the Austrian-administered duchy of Holstein.

Although Frankfurt had refrained from taking an active part in the war, Prussian troops occupied and annexed the Free City, bringing to an end its traditional role as the unofficial capital of the German federation. The seat of power shifted in fact as well as in name to Berlin, and Frankfurt, no longer a Free City nor an imperial one, was degraded to the status of a provincial Prussian center. No sooner had the Prussian armies entered the city than Commanding General von Falckenstein dissolved the city government and General von Manteuffel, who commanded the Army of the Main, demanded the payment of 25 million florins—about ten million dollars —as a war contribution inside 24 hours.

Lord Mayor Viktor Fellner committed suicide in a fit of despondency over the city's occupation and the exorbitant demands of the Prussian generals. Citizens of Frankfurt also considered it a bad omen that the four-hundred-year-old cathedral was gutted by fire the day Prussia's

Prussian General von Manteuffel demands 25 million florins inside 24 hours as a war contribution from the City of Frankfurt, 1866.

sovereign, William I, paid the first visit to his new subjects in 1867.

It seemed somehow ominous and symbolic of Frankfurt's decline that the church bells which had rung in the fairs, coronations and assemblies typical of the city's life for hundreds of years, melted away in the conflagration. In the minds of many a citizen the future of Frankfurt looked glum indeed at this point.

But the cathedral was presently restored according to the original plans of architect Madern Gertener drawn up in 1415. The steeple provided for in the Gertener plans but never completed was added to the tower, and new bells, more ponderous than the old were installed in the belfry. The largest of the bells, christened 'Gloriosa', weighed 13 tons. It was fashioned from the metal of its predecessors and that of French guns captured in the Franco-Prussian War of 1871.

Frankfurt began to adjust itself to its new fate and Bismarck proceeded with astute moderation in converting the former seat of the commonwealth to a Prussian provincial center. By selecting the city as the site for concluding the Franco-Prussian peace treaty of 1871, the first major foreign policy move of the new German Empire headed by Prussia, he went a long way towards soothing the sensibilities of leading citizens. Once more the name of Frankfurt was linked with a major event in German history. Economic prosperity, the attainment of German unity, and the frequent polite nods in the direction of Frankfurt's imperial tradition by the central government in Berlin, served to reconcile the majority of Frankfurters to their new status as Prussian subjects.

The nearly unbridled expansion of Frankfurt in the latter nineteenth century is evidenced by its population increase from 85,000 in 1871 to 375,000 by 1910. With tax returns showing 600 millionaires among Frankfurt's population at that time, most of them patrons of the arts and sciences as well as contributors to the city's social welfare projects, there was little to complain about in the years preceding the first world war.

THE NEW FRANKFURT

The magnitude of the task faced by city planners in building up the new Frankfurt at once becomes apparent when one considers that of 177,000 apartments in the city, only 44,000 remained intact after World War II. From this three-quarter destruction of habitable housing units, Frankfurt bounced back to a level of 185,000 apartments by 1957, and to almost 300,000 by the mid-1970's.

It took considerable courage to reconstruct the city entirely on modern lines. Practically nothing was left of the old town when post-war reconstruction started, but as the old quarter was considered a jewel of medieval architecture, the tradition-minded would have liked to see the winding streets rebuilt and lined as before with narrow, gabled buildings.

Instead, the city government named in the first free post-war elections of early 1946, decided to build functional apartment and office buildings on the site of old Frankfurt. Streets were widened and straightened, bringing sunlight, greenery and a new concept of spaciousness to the twisted lanes littered with wreckage. Reconstruction in the original style was confined to less than a half dozen historic buildings, among them the city hall and Goethe's birthplace. A broad new avenue — Berliner Strasse — flanked by gleaming surfaces of glass, steel and whitewashed concrete, lays a ribbon of asphalt across what was once the heart of the old city, and the area between city hall and cathedral, the "Römerberg", formerly host of a hundred streets, back alleys and courtyards, is now an open mall covering an underground parking lot and a subway station, and hosting numerous carnivals and fairs. These include the annual Christmas Market and the so-called 'Day of the Open Door', an annual autumn "open house" festival featuring open air stage performances, concerts and folkloric presentations, and honoring delegations from Frankfurt's sister cities of Birmingham, Lyon and Milan.

The reconstruction of the Römerberg presented the city with the opportunity to excavate and put on display in a historical garden the remains of Roman and early medieval structures.

The Römerberg has become the site of free debates, children's treasure hunts, chess games and wurststands. In the 20th century it is becoming a focal point of civic activities, reminiscent of its historic position of earlier centuries. Some city architects would like to see modern buildings rise between the Römer and the Cathedral. But even some of the more progressive-minded civic leaders recognize the advantages of maintaining the traditional and historic mood of Old Frankfurt. It remains to be seen whether sentimentality will win out over practicality on the Römerberg.

But an indication of the current trend has been the establishment of a commission to identify historic buildings and areas within the city and to protect them as city monuments. Designated buildings qualify for facelifting, subsidised to a greater or lesser degree by the city.

Since World War II, private business poured millions into construction effort, creating modern department stores, super-markets and an entertainment industry reflecting the city's role as a focal point of commerce and industry. Financing of new construction project by the more than 200 banks and credit associations that make Frankfurt the nation's financial capital, brought to the scene many an audacious project of American proportions.

The new Frankfurt has the enterprising face of an American city. Contractors and businessmen have been quick to adapt to the community's need methods and products evolved in the U. S. A. to make life more comfortable for the average family.

Self-service food stores and supermarkets dominate local shopping habits. The upsurge in production and sale of home refrigerators attesting to the steady rise in living standards, is transforming food buying habits in ways paralleling the American experience; fewer trips to the store, more items bought each time. Major department stores are also adopting the 'come-in-and-browse-around' concept in favor of the traditional 'what-can-I-show-you'. The sales clerk dogging your footsteps has been replaced by attractive packing and an advertising industry growing each year as an off-shoot of Madison Avenue. American-style drug stores, ice cream stands, fried chicken restaurants and hotels bearing familiar American names have appeared much to the delight of some, and to the dismay of other more romantically inclined citizens and visitors.

Automation has emerged full-blown in mid-century Frankfurt. The Opel plant in nearby Ruesselsheim, a subsidiary of General Motors, and A.E.G., the largest German utility company, affiliated with General Electric, are pioneers in this field. Particularly ingenious is the municipal sewage disposal method, a self-contained and fully automatic system breaking down foul sewer waters into odorless artificial fertilizer for neighborhood farmers and cooking gas for the city's housewives. The three egg-shaped tanks used in the conversion process are an eyestopper on the road to the airport.

Prosperity has brought congestion to the streets of the city. Despite an elaborate system of traffic signals spaced with German thoroughness at halfblock intervals along busy streets, traffic tie-ups are frequent during the rush hour. Efforts to relieve the parking problem were crowned by a number of municipal parking houses, each providing space for several hundred cars. Within easy walking distance of the main shopping areas, the parking houses come equipped with garage service facilities. Parking meters line the main avenues, providing a welcome extra source of revenue for the city administration. With more people than ever before owning cars and many of them not yet quite used to it, safe driving habits and the lack of same are a favorite subject of foreign tourists, traffic police and editorial self-chastisement on the local pages of the daily papers. There is a reason: Germany's traffic accident rate is one of the highest in Europe.

Technical improvements are the drawing cards of a lively campaign to step up business and vacationers' use of the federal railways; streamlined, air-conditioned diesel coaches, cruising along at nearly 90 mph, are part of the *Trans-Europe Express* system now linking Frankfurt with the continent's major cities. Slow-moving river steamers provide the other end on the scale of effort to get the traveler off the highways. The Rhein-Main steamship system with Frankfurt as its terminus, connects with all German waterways. If time is no object and sight-seeing the main consideration, this is an ideal way to travel. Ships depart practically at the foot of the city hall; the river port and industrial dockyards with their 110 miles of track the largest in Germany, are located some distance away along the city's eastern outskirts.

In 1968, after five years of construction, the first stretch of Frankfurt's "U-Bahn" or subway system was opened. By the mid-1980's the system will consist of a network of some 90 miles of U-Bahn tracks, including 25 miles of tunnels. The system will interconnect with an additional 250 miles of Federal German Railway "S-Bahn" or rapid transit commuter system, connecting Frankfurt with cities as far away as Wiesbaden, Hanau, Darmstadt, and Friedberg. The inauguration of the U-Bahn in 1968 coincided with the opening of the "Nordweststadt-Zentrum", which was hailed as a model community center.

In an effort to encourage commuters to use the subway system, and thus reduce traffic congestion, city fathers provided free parking areas at strategic locations near U-Bahn stations around the city, modeled after the "park and ride" programs of many American cities.

The hub of the entire public transit system is of course the Hauptbahnhof, or main railway station which, while maintaining its exterior facade, will be completely rebuilt within to include S-Bahn and U-Bahn stations, as well as parking for hundreds of automobiles.

The new Frankfurt has increasingly turned into a center of scientific research. Of international repute is the Max Planck Institute of Biophysics attached to the

University, and the Gmelin Institute, an international documentation center that does for chemistry what the Academie Francaise accomplishes for the French language: defining new concepts, and keeping current an ever expanding encyclopedia of chemical knowledge the world over. Germany's equivalent of the Library of Congress, the 'Deutsche Bibliothek,' has also moved to Frankfurt and completed cataloguing its initial stock of a quarter million books. A sixteen story structure houses the library which aims eventually to obtain a copy of every book and magazine published in the German language.

An important guide-post to the significance of Frankfurt's technological present and future is the Battelle Institute, located at the west edge of the city near the fairgrounds. An non-profit foundation originally organized in Columbus, Ohio, Battelle undertakes applied research in all fields under contract to private business firms and industrial organizations. The institute enables private firms to farm out all or part of their new product development, smoothing the road towards better products and higher living standards. Research is currently underway at the institute in nuclear reactor safety.

The Frankfurt of the mid 1970's has become the financial and trade capital of Germany, if not of Europe. Predestined to that fate after World War II by the polarization of Europe, and by its strategic position as the crossroads of communication and transportation, it regained the position it lost to Berlin in the late 19th century.

Recognizing the potential, city planners encouraged development in this direction. On all sides are indications of this development. High-rise office buildings, banks and hotels change the skyline almost daily. Foreign trade missions, and corporations and banks with foreign names are all signs of Frankfurt's significance in the world of trade. The city has become the address of the home offices of many leading German and international industries, with the factories themselves located elsewhere. The importance of the Rhein-Main airport as one of the main gateways to Europe has made the tourist industry an important segment of Frankfurt's industry. At the center of this activity, of course, is the Frankfurt stock exchange, which is second only to London as Europe's indicator of the economic pulse of the world. Also significant to Frankfurt's position as a trade center are the grain exchange, the gold exchange, and the newly opened diamond exchange.

A description of Frankfurt today would be incomplete without mention of Frankfurt as a mecca of music. Thanks to the Century Hall (Jahrhunderthalle) in suburban Hoechst, and the Festhalle at the Fairgrounds, which have a combined capacity of over 10,000, there is hardly a jazz, rock, or pop musician of note who has not performed in Frankfurt. The city hosts the German Jazz Festival, 3 days in length, every two years. In existance since 1951, it is the oldest regularly held jazz festival in the world.

Jazz in Frankfurt actually had its beginnings during the war years. Influenced by English and American popular music heard during the late 30's on Radio Luxembourg, and by French music after the German occupation of France, young local musicians sought out others with similar interests. Carlo Bohlaender, Emil Mangelsdorff, Hans-Otto Jung and Horst Lippmann opened the "Hot Club Frankfurt" in a back room club on Kaiserstrasse where they played "Swing", as they called the new sounds. On the signal from a lookout that the police or Gestapo were nearby, the "Swing" changed to German march and patriotic music. When the coast was clear, the "decadent" jazz filled the room once again. After the war, Bohlaender, Lippmann and Mangelsdorff went on to become leading jazz musicians of Germany. And the German Jazz Festival of today is a direct descendant of the "Hot Club Frankfurt". The large number of Americans stationed around Frankfurt had more to do with the city's becoming a center of jazz and pop music than most people recognize. Especially in the immediate post war years, American servicemen, hungry for familiar stateside music, flocked to the jazz cellars and concerts and created the climate in which this music was able to thrive. In recent years such American and English stars of the popular music world as Liza Minelli, The Carpenters, Aritha Franklin, Frank Sinatra, Jethro Tull, as well as the late Jimmi Hendrix and Janis Joplin, have appeared in Frankfurt.

The oldest view of Frankfurt, 1492.

Famous Frankfurters

Johann Wolfgang von Goethe, 1749-1832

Without a doubt, Frankfurt's greatest son was Johann Wolfgang von Goethe, poet laureate of the German-speaking world. A universal genius, Goethe excelled equally as a playwright, scientist and statesman. His dramas had as much impact on German life and literature as those of Shakespeare and Marlowe on the development of the English-speaking peoples. Goethe's collected works fill about 143 volumes, and a hundred thousand books devoted to the poet and his influence on European society line the walls of the Goethe Museum adjoining his Frankfurt birthplace. Perhaps best known among his works outside of Germany is the monumental two-part drama 'Faust', depicting man's age-old quest for knowledge and power, the biographical novel 'The Sufferings of Young Werther', and the poet's memoirs in a volume titled 'Truth and Poetry'.

Goethe was born on Grosser Hirschgraben 23 on the memorable 28th of August 1749. His well-to-do parents, lawyer Johann Kaspar Goethe and his beautiful young wife Elizabeth, daughter of Frankfurt mayor Johann Wolfgang Textor, gave their talented son all the advantages of a liberal education. Besides his native German, young Goethe learned to talk six foreign languages while still a boy and at the age of 12 was required to write his father seven letters weekly in seven different tongues.

Entering Leipzig University at the age of 16, he had no difficulty in following lectures on philology, law and philosophy, most of them delivered in Latin. Following in the footsteps of his father, young Goethe traveled widely to complete his education.

As a boy Goethe witnessed the coronation of Emperor Joseph II, an event that provided one of his strongest early impressions. He managed to secure a place on the stairs leading up to the Kaisersaal where he could see the emperor, the electors and the other princes at close range when they arrived for the coronation banquet. A steward handed the well-dressed lad a dish for the Emperor's table and young Wolfgang thus got a glimpse of the historic scene, described vividly some sixty years later in his memoirs.

After finishing his university studies at Leipzig and Strasbourg, Goethe returned to his family home and spent the next years in Frankfurt. Here he wrote his first volumes of poetry, the historical drama 'Goetz von Berlichingen' and the original version of his latter-day masterpiece, 'Faust'. Goethe's genius thrived on romantic attachments and most of his contemporaries forgave a disregard of social conventions that would have made life difficult for a lesser man. The women in the poet's life obtained immortality in idealized form on page after page of his staggering literary outpouring. Putting creative freedom above the gilded cage of family ties, Goethe broke off his engagement with Lili Schoenemann, daughter of a Frankfurt banker, and followed a call to the Weimar court of Duke Charles August in 1775. He remained there till the end of his days.

Young Goethe, portrait by Georg Melchior Kraus in the Goethe Museum, Frankfurt.

Monument to Johann Wolfgang von Goethe by sculptor Ludwig Schwan-
thaler unveiled in 1844, twelve years after the poet's death (Gallus-Anlage).

Monument to the poet Heinrich Heine by Georg Kolbe, erected 1913 in the
Taunus-Anlage, a garden promenade occupying the site of the city's inner
belt of moats and fortifications razed in the early 19th century.

Samuel Thomas von Soemmering (1755-1830).
Inventor of the electric telegraph.

Arthur Schopenhauer (1788-1860).
Early photograph by C. F. Mylius.

Paul Ehrlich (1854-1915).
Nobel Prize Winner.

Johann Christian Senckenberg (1707-1772).
Dr. med., physician and founder.

Aiding the sovereign in the administration of his small duchy, and concentrating on his writing and studies which also gave birth to essays on archeology, botany, chemistry and zoology, Goethe led a full and satisfying life at Weimar. Many-splendored were his attachments to the literate women of his day, expressed in a correspondence that mirrors the eternal elation and exhaustion of passion in the search for kindred spirits.

He married his companion, Christiane Vulpius seventeen years after she bore him a son, but even in late years his passions pursued him. As a man of 65, he was inspired to some of the greatest love poems in world literature by the 31-year-old wife of a Frankfurt banker, Marianne von Willemer. The daughter of Austrian showpeople, Marianne was adopted, raised with his children and later married by Willemer, 25 years her senior. She met Goethe when the poet returned to Frankfurt in 1814, and their sentimental attachment, tolerated by Willemer, inspired the pair to write couplets of an allegorical oriental style giving vent to desire, self-abnegation and wisdom. Goethe later published this collection of poems under the title, 'West-Eastern Divan'. The mellowed stanzas are ripe with resignation. Universal as the range of his interests, Goethe's erudition was proverbial among his contemporaries. He spoke fluent Italian, a language he loved to use. He talked to Napoleon in French and addressed Carlyle in English. As an old man he took up the study of Oriental languages and Balkan folkways. He learned Hebrew as a boy in order to read the old testament in the original, acquired early Greek and Coptic to study the texts of the scriptures.

Goethe's study at Grosser Hirschgraben 23.

Goethe followed closely developments in the expanding United States. 'It's worth the effort to gaze into a world in growth', he jotted in his notebooks after acquiring a number of U. S. publications while working on the novel 'Wilhelm Meister's Travel Years' in the 1820'. A few years earlier, Goethe had presented several volumes of his works to the Harvard University Library, with the handwritten flyleaf entry: "Gift of the author, Joh. Wolfgang Goethe of Germany." He read the novels of James Fenimore Cooper with "much admiration" and received U. S. historian George Bancroft—later ambassador to Germany—and scientist Joseph Green Cogswell in 1817. Into this period falls Goethe's poem extolling the fresh approach and unburdened outlook of the new country. It runs:

> '*Amerika du hast es besser*
> *Als unser Kontinent der Alte*
> *Hast keine verfallenen Schloesser*
> *Und keine Basalte*
> *Dich stoert nicht im Innern*
> *Zu lebendiger Zeit*
> *Unnuetzes Erinnern*
> *Und vergeblicher Streit.*'

(America your lot is facile / compare this continent the old / you've got no dilapidated castles / no cult of the mold / not burdened internally / throughout your days / by superfluous memory / and futile frays.)

In memory of the poet, the city of Frankfurt awards a Goethe Prize once every three years to creative workers in all fields of human endeavor. Their accomplishments must permit them to meet the eyes of Goethe without flinching. The award is presented on the day and hour of Goethe's birth—12 noon, August 28th. Since the initial presentation in 1927, the list of recipients has included men like Sigmund Freud, Thomas Mann, Max Planck and Albert Schweitzer.

Paul Ehrlich, Nobel Prize Winner, Discoverer of Salvarsan

The man who freed mankind from the scourge of syphilis was the school example of the absent-minded professor. Paul Ehrlich's laboratory in Frankfurt's Speyer foundation was so cluttered that no visitor could take advantage of the courteous invitation to sit down which the scholar never failed to voice. He smoked 25 cigars a day, carried his medals and decorations around on his travels in an old cigar box and was known for his fabulous memory of past experiments with which he continually stumped his associates. After putting arsenic through 605 combinations on a scientific hunch that tested his perseverance in a sheer endless series of experiments aimed at combatting the syphilis-causing spirochete, 'Combination 606' proved effective in stopping the previously incurable, often fatal venereal disease.

Millions of people saw the professor's search for the wonder drug re-enacted by Paul Muni in the prize-winning film of the early forties, titled 'Dr. Ehrlich's Magic Bullet'. The scientist used to get his best ideas while listening to light music and tipped street musicians handsomely to crank their organs beneath his office window. Associates recall that the professor maintained the ordered confusion of his laboratory by telling charwomen all his books and papers were soaked in a poison against which he alone was immune. Another time, Ehrlich bent on explaining a new experiment to a visiting scientist, scribbled chemical formulas on the backs of picture postcards while eating lunch at a Frankfurt restaurant. As soon as he covered a card with the chemical symbols, he would throw it on the floor and reach for a new one. At the end of the meal, the headwaiter carefully gathered up the scribbled notes and presented the perplexed professor with a bill for five dozen picture postcards.

When he decided to move here from Danzig in 1831, philosopher Arthur Schopenhauer jotted in his journal: 'Advantages of Frankfurt—healthy climate, nice scenery, amenities of large city, the Natural History Museum, better plays, operas and concerts, more Englishmen, better coffee houses, no bad water, the Senckenberg library, no floods, a capable dentist and not too many bad doctors, no unbearable heat in summer, you are watched less, you are more independent and at liberty to avoid disagreeable company.' The famous bachelor lived and worked here until his death in 1860, providing by his odd behavior the subject of innumerable anecdotes. Schopenhauer preferred the company of his poodle whom he called Atman —Sanskrit for world soul—to that of humans, would gesticulate and talk wildly to himself on his daily walks to and from the Hotel Englischer Hof where he took his meals.

Schopenhauer resented people, social conventions and the gaping curiosity with which visitors regarded the great non-conformist. His caustic remarks were legion, but he likewise was capable of a singular devotion. Rossini was his favorite composer. The philosopher would never miss one of his operas and he termed the works of all other composers clumsy by comparison. Once the Italian maestro stopped at the Englischer Hof and the maitre d'hotel pointed out the new arrival to his admirer, volunteering to introduce them. Schopenhauer who sat only two tables away, regarded the composer critically, then muttered with a disappointed shrug: "This man can never be Rossini; he's just a fat Frenchman."

In making out his testament, he provided amply for his poodle and specified that the grave marker read merely 'Arthur Schopenhauer'. When asked if the had any preferences for a final resting place, he replied testily 'if anyone wants me, he will find me'.

Samuel Thomas von Soemmering, Inventor of the Electric Telegraph

Told about Doctor Soemmering's strange instrument for transmitting electrical impulses by wire, Napoleon thought for a moment about its possible military application, then dismissed it as an impractical *'idee germanique'*. But in the form later perfected by Samuel F. B. Morse, the electromagnetic device ushered in a new age of communication linking countries and continents at the touch of a fingertip. Twenty eight years divide Soemmering's crude telegraph of 1809 from the Morse version made public in 1837. In the interval, the Frankfurt physician who tinkered as a hobby with electrical equipment reaped honors for his anatomical discoveries. He popularized the smallpox vaccination, was knighted and died without ever seeing the communications tool he devised in a spare moment start its conquest of the world. Elisabeth Soemmering, the doctor's wife, was a talented painter of miniatures and the couple were good friends of the Goethe family. Goethe was their house guest while Soemmering taught at Mainz university, and the poet noted in his journals that he breathed hometown air on his return from France in the house of 'the one and only Betty'.

In case anyone should have the notion Alexander Graham Bell invented the telephone, Frankfurt historians will be quick to point out that Philipp Reis demonstrated his battery-operated device called a 'telephone' before the Frankfurt physics association, October 26, 1861. An improved version was put by Reis before the physical science convention at Giessen in 1864. Alex Bell didn't get moving on his claim until 1878. Born in the nearby French Huguenot village of Friedrichsdorf, Reis, who earned his living as a science teacher, moved to Frankfurt in 1850 and worked here on his electrical inventions. He was only forty years old when he died, broken by his complete failure to get industrialists interested in mass production of the new invention, hailed by magazines as a sensation and described in detail by the scientific publications of the period.

A monument near the Eschenheimer tower showing two youths having a telephone conversation—for reasons known only to the sculptor they are nude—and a street behind the fair grounds, perpetuate the memory of the scientific pioneer ignored during his lifetime.

A generation after Reis first demonstrated the telephone, Frankfurt manufacturers developed an interest in 'electro-technical' innovations, going so far as to sponsor the International Electro-technical Exhibit of 1891. Main attraction of the show was the world's first long-distance high voltage transmission. A 300 hp turbine in Lauffen am Neckar generated 15,000 volts, relayed to the fairgrounds by landline over a distance of 110 miles. The turbine's output powered a thousand lamps and the pumps of an artificial waterfall, providing the first proof that overland transmission of high voltage alternating current was both possible and economical.

Rudolf Christian Boettger, Inventor of Gun Cotton and the Safety Match

Benefactor of countless smokers and housewives by his invention of the safety match, Professor Boettger also aided demolition experts, photographers and physicians with varied uses for the gun cotton he devised. Known as collodion, the ether-treated substance obtained wide applications in photography and as an antiseptic for wounds.

Boettger, who lived in Frankfurt from 1842 until his death at 75 in 1881, is also credited with a host of other discoveries among them the process of nickelplating and the reproduction of copper engravings. He found time to father eight children of whom one, Oskar Boettger (1848-1910) became a noted zoologist. Out of sheer modesty, Boettger never used the hereditary knighthood bestowed on him by the Austrian Emperor in 1853. A revealing personal glimpse of the scientist is given in the obituary published by the chemical society: 'Professor Boettger used to get up regularly at 4 o'clock in the morning and wind all the clocks in his house while making his first cup of coffee. When the family joined him at the breakfast table he already had several hours of work behind him. Most of his life he knew only one walk, from his house to his laboratory where he worked mornings and afternoons, including Sundays. In his last years he enjoyed sitting afternoons in the Palmengarten, listening to band concerts while taking up research problems with his friends and associates over coffee and cigars.'

Hoffmann and Humperdinck

Why the author of the world's most famous children's book and the composer of the best-known children's opera happened to occupy adjoining apartments at Grueneburg-weg 95 during the last decade of the 19th century is a question the goddess of coincidence alone can answer. The fact remains that Heinrich Hoffmann, who put his un-kempt, nasty 'Struwwelpeter' through a series of dire pre-dicaments as a warning to countless little boys, and the composer of 'Haensel and Gretel', Engelbert Humperdinck were next-door neighbors in a nondescript gray apartment house, just a stone's throw from the Farben building.

Struwwelpeter.

A memorial tablet unveiled on the 100th anniversary of Hoffmann's birth in 1954 re-calls the joint occupancy for the occasional passerby who happens to glance up the front of the unassuming dwelling. Hoffmann was 80 years old when his 36 year-old neighbor Humperdinck wrote the opera based on the Grimm brothers fairytale of two children lost in the magic forest. Now translated into 17 languages, Haensel and Gretel had its premiere in Weimar under the baton of Richard Strauss shortly before the turn of the century and has since been taken over into the repertory of major opera companies throughout the world, including New York's Metropolitan, for traditional Christmas performances.

While Humperdinck was a full-time composer, music teacher and critic, Hoffmann wrote his world-famous children's books, 'Struwwelpeter' and 'The Nutcracker' as a lark to amuse his sons and daughters. In private life, Hoffmann was the head doctor of the municipal insane asylum—known as the Affenstein—located on the grounds later occupied by the Farben building. The original manuscript of Hoffmann's 'Struwwelpeter' was acquired by the city of Frankfurt from a rare book dealer in the USA several years ago. Humperdinck's scores of Haensel and Gretel, voluminous personal diaries, covering the 42 years of his productive life, manuscripts and correspondence, are also in the city's possession, a still unexplored treasure trove for the historian and musicologist.

* * *

Kurt Debus, Space Scientist

Probably the Frankfurter best known to Americans in recent years is Dr. Kurt Debus, who retired in 1974 after serving as the director of the John F. Kennedy Space Center since 1963. Born in Frankfurt in 1908, at Guenthersburgallee 18, he received his education in the Liebig School in Frankfurt. He was working as a research scientist in the field of aerodynamics at the Darmstadt Technical College shortly before World War II when he met Wernherr von Braun. He spent the war years with von Braun and his staff at Peenemuende, where the V-series of rockets were developed. After the war Dr. Debus and Wernherr von Braun along with many other scientists continued their rocket research at Fort Bliss, Texas; White Sands Missile Range, New Mexico; and later at Huntsville, Alabama and Cape Canaveral, Florida, in the meantime becoming a citizen of the United States. In 1973, during the Hoechster Schlossfest, Dr. Debus was interviewed live via satellite from his office in Florida by a panel of German and American journalists and young scientists who were attending the festival in the Frankfurt suburb of Hoechst.

* * *

Noted among the outstanding men and women who made Frankfurt their home in recent years are the author Alfons Paquet, composer Paul Hindemith and conductor Georg Solti, painter Max Beckmann, public servant Walter Kolb Frankfurt's late Lord Mayor, radiologist Friedrich Dessauer and biophysicist Boris Rajewsky.

We already know about the Holy Roman Emperors and will soon read about noted American's who stayed in Frankfurt. Here are some other notables whose visits to the city are worth recalling:

A clammy November week over a hundred fifty years ago saw Napoleon and the three sovereigns who pursued his retreating forces after the battle of Leipzig, pass through Frankfurt in rapid succession. Tsar Alexander of Russia, Emperor Francis of Austria, and King Frederick William III. of Prussia led the allied field forces numbering some 80,000 men in a triumphal march straight through the city. While Napoleon retreated across the Rhine and fruitless armistice negotiations dragged on for weeks, most of the allied force had to be billeted in the city. Frankfurters who had breathed a sigh of relief when Napoleon diverted his starved army around the city after spending the night of October 31st in the villa of banker von Bethmann, now had to face epidemics, requisitions and the shortages brought on by the temporary doubling of the population.

* * *

Painter Albrecht Duerer visited here with art patron, merchant and mayor Jakob Heller in July 1520. Some years earlier, Heller had commissioned the artist to paint the Thomas altar for the Dominican church—the altar is still preserved in the Historical Museum—and Duerer came here to call on his benefactor, accompanied by his wife Agnes. Tradition has it that Duerer's wife, on other occasions, sold the artist's drawings in the Christmas market on Roemerberg square.

* * *

Tourists visiting Frankfurt before the war often went away with the impression that Martin Luther had spent some days in a tiny weatherbeaten house facing the cathedral. The place was known as 'Luther's corner' and prominently displayed a picture of the reformer over the main entrance. Actually Luther, who was in Frankfurt two nights in April 1521 on the way to and from the defense of his doctrine at the diet of Worms, stayed in the nearby Gasthaus of Wolf Parente, a building torn down in 1896. His picture was placed many years later on the house facing the cathedral for the sole purpose of annoying Roman Catholic clerics who had to pass by 'Luther's corner' daily.

* * *

Excerpt from a letter by Felix Mendelssohn, dated Frankfurt, July 14, 1836: "... am sitting here in the corner room, overlooking the Main. The view is enviable, looking downstream in this lovely summer weather and watching the passage of the ships and barges. On the shore across, my old favorite the watchtower pointing South and on the other side, the blue mountains; I came here with great plans to work, but now almost a week has passed and I have done little else in the morning but sun myself and admire the view. Will probably keep loafing another few days ...". Mendelssohn was a frequent visitor and married a Frankfurt girl. He composed several of his *lieder* for open air festivals in the city forest.

* * *

Wolfgang Amadeus Mozart gave four concerts in Frankfurt, the first three as a 'Wunderkind' of seven in August 1763, the last during the coronation festivities of 1790 when he was a penniless composer of 34, already marked by death. Father Leopold Mozart and his twelve year old sister Nannerl accompanied the young genius who amused a Frankfurt audience by playing his compositions from memory on a violin, piano and organ with a cloth-covered keyboard, improvising on any given tune. Because of the success of the first concert on August 18th, father Leopold arranged two more performances for his youngsters on the 22nd and 30th of the month before continuing on his concert tour of the continent. He also found time to scratch into the window pane at his boarding house on Bendergasse 3: "Mozart Maitre de la Musique de la Chapelle de Salzbourg avec sa famille le 12 Aout 1763."

Twenty-seven years later his famous son, now in bad health and plagued as usual by financial difficulties, once again undertook the strenuous coach trip from Vienna to seek income from a recital in the city crowded with spectators for the coronation of Leopold II. The trip, Mozart wrote to his wife, 'took only six days'. He also noted 'I am liked and admired certainly, but what one hears about imperial cities is a lot of boasting; the people here are pennypinchers even worse than in Vienna'.

Unfortunately the concert on October 15th confirmed Mozart's suspicions; there was 'much honor, but little money', since a parade and a princely banquet staged that same day drew off part of his prospective audience. Even those present began to leave after the intermission,

Mit gnädigster Erlaubniß

Wird Heute Freytags den 15ten October 1790.

im grosen Stadt-Schauspielhause

Herr Kapellmeister Mozart

ein groses

musikalisches Konzert

zu seinem Vortheil geben.

Erster Theil.

Eine neue grose Simphonie von Herrn Mozart.

Eine Arie, gesungen von Madame Schick.

Ein Concert auf dem Forte-piano, gespielt von Herrn Kapellmeister Mozart von seiner eigenen Komposition.

Eine Arie, gesungen von Herrn Cecarelli.

Zweyter Theil.

Ein Konzert von Herrn Kapellmeister Mozart von seiner eigenen Komposition.

Ein Duett, gesungen von Madame Schick und Herrn Cecarelli.

Eine Phantasie aus dem Stegreife von Herrn Mozart.

Eine Symphonie.

Die Person zahlt in den Logen und Parquet 2 fl. 45 kr.

Auf der Gallerie 24 kr.

Billets sind bey Herrn Mozart, wohnhaft in der Kahlbechergasse Nro. 167. vom Donnerstag Nachmittags und Freytags Frühe bey Herrn Cassirer Scheidweiler und an der Casse zu haben.

Der Anfang ist um Eilf Uhr Vormittags.

A poster announcing Mozart's playing his own compositions in Frankfurt, October 15, 1790.

forcing him to cancel the last number of the recital, which was originally scheduled to last about three hours.

* * *

In 1922, Pope Pius XII, then Papal Nuncio Eugenio Pacelli, accompanied by Cardinal Faulhaber of Munich and Bishop Keppeler of Rottenburg looked at the rooms occupied in the Schopenhauer house, adjoining the present site of the city library, by catholic savant Johannes Janssen. Professor Janssen, a catholic prelate, taught at the city high school and was the author of a monumental tome on the German reformation from the catholic view. He died in his study on Christmas Eve 1891.

* * *

Voltaire was arrested at the inn to the Golden Lion here in 1753. Confinement of the French philosopher whose satire 'Candide' ranks among the world's greatest literary accomplishments, was ordered by King Frederick of Prussia. The Prussian king and the French satirist were known for their frequent quarrels, interspersed with spells of mutual admiration. Voltaire was detained in order to recover a collection of poems by the king containing satires on several princes, some of which Voltaire was said to have exhibited maliciously at the courts of Europe.

* * *

The influx of crowned heads into nearby Bad Homburg late in the last century brought the sovereigns of England, Russia and even Siam to the metropolis on the Main. The railway station, built in 1888, boasted a separate 'reception room for princes.' No doubt it held an illustrious assembly when King Umberto of Italy strode in at precisely 7.30 in the morning of May 26, 1889 to lead his retinue to the waiting carriages. The station square was blocked off by troops and special tickets were issued to enable the privileged citizens shown in the old newspaper photograph to watch the spectacle.

The passing parade through Frankfurt's railway station also included Edward VII of Great Britain to whom we are indebted for the 'Homburg', originated during the 32 successive years he vacationed and dieted at the nearby spa. Sources have it that Bad Homburg masseurs and rigid dieting relieved him annually of as much as 40 pounds. Conservatively this exceeds a thousand royal pounds in a lifetime.

The Russian Orthodox chapel in Bad Homburg, dedicated by Tsar Nicholas II in 1899.

A special attraction in Bad Homburg is the Russian orthodox chapel, which was dedicated September 22, 1899 during a visit of Tsar Nicholas II of the Russias and his Tsarina, Alexandra.

Pagoda donated by King Chulalongkorn of Siam to Bad Homburg, 1907.

A few years later King Chulalongkorn of Siam invited all of Bad Homburg to a buffet when he dedicated the pagoda put up in the municipal park as his donation to the city. It was the monarch's way of celebrating his 57th birthday, September 22, 1907.

* * *

Louis and François Blanc, Churchill, Dostoyevsky, Duse, Liszt and Wagner are some of the other names that lived in and passed through Frankfurt and its environs in the quiet days before World War I. The famous Blanc twins, small-town bankers in Bordeaux, founded their immense wealth on the blinking of a semaphor that relayed Paris stock exchange quotations to the enterprising brothers, days before their competitors obtained the news via courier riders. In 1841 they built the gambling casino in Bad Homburg which François operated until his death in 1877. François likewise took over the run-down Monte Carlo casino in 1863 and made this Riviera spot a rendezvous of the international gambling and social set which it has remained to this day.

* * *

Winston Spencer Churchill, one of the world's great statesmen who as a historian had the rare advantage of making the history he wrote about, visited Frankfurt while serving as Britain's home secretary shortly before World War I. Eleonora Duse, the Italian actress who thrilled three generations was there in 1894; Franz Liszt, like his son-in-law Richard Wagner who came to Frankfurt to conduct Tannhaeuser and Lohengrin in 1862, were frequent visitors to the city.

* * *

Famous Americans who have visited Frankfurt include Thomas Jefferson, Benjamin Franklin, Mrs. Mary Todd Lincoln, who lived in Frankfurt for 5 years with her son Tad after Lincoln's assassination, former President Ulysses S. Grant and Presidents Harry S. Truman, Dwight D. Eisenhower and John F. Kennedy.

SIGHTS OF THE CITY

The Airport (number 22 on map)

It seems fitting somehow that Frankfurt airport became the first civil jet airport in Germany; the city has always been air-minded. As a matter of fact, Frankfurt's first airport came into use in 1909, and the calendar showed October 3, 1785 when man first stepped into space over Frankfurt. It was an intrepid Frenchman, Jean Pierre Blanchard, whose exploits in ascending with a gas-filled balloon to a height of six thousand feet above Frankfurt are immortalized in old engravings and eyewitness reports preserved among municipal documents. Blanchard covered the thirty mile stretch between Frankfurt and Weilburg in 39 minutes, landing safely in the garden of the local palace after the stunt of dropping a dog by parachute over Frankfurt's outskirts with a note pinned to his harness asking the finder to deliver the pet to the Frenchman's hotel.

Within five years after the Wright Brothers had ushered in the air age by their historic flight at Kitty Hawk, the home-made planes of German air pioneers were hopskipping above Rebstock airstrip at the edge of the city, next to the Wiesbaden road. This was also the terrain chosen for the International Air Travel Exposition from July to October 1909 at which some 400 exhibitors displayed their latest aviation products. The catalogue included the

Wright Brothers German subsidiary 'Flugmaschine Wright Gesellschaft, Berlin'.

Rhein Main airport, six miles south of the city, was the home base of Germany's giant dirigibles before the war. From here the 'Hindenburg' took off for her ill-fated flight to Lakehurst, New Jersey in May 1937. Thirty six passengers and crew members perished in the disaster that spelled the end of the lighter-than-air craft as a means of transatlantic transportation. But many, including a number of dirigible veterans who live in the nearby suburb of Zeppelinheim, believe that the end of the airship is not yet. With its round-the-world range and facilities for several hundred passengers, the dirigible provides an ideal means for inexpensive long-distance transportation. And safety can be assured by using non-flammable helium, now available in ample quantities, instead of the highly-combustible hydrogen that doomed the Hindenburg.

Since the opening of the new Frankfurt terminal in March 1972 the Frankfurt airport rapidly achieved top ranking among European airports. Today it is first in terms of mail, second in terms of air freight and third, after Heathrow and Orly, in numbers of passengers, with over 12 million annually. There is hardly a minute, day or night, when the terminal is not humming with activity. The main advantage of Frankfurt Rhein-Main airport is its convenient geographical location in the heart of Europe, as evidenced by the unusually high percentage of passengers who transfer at Frankfurt. Over 60 airlines connect Frankfurt with nearly 200 cities in 90 countries.

The new terminal includes a railway station beneath the main concourse, with frequent direct connections to Frankfurt and Mainz. A traveler might depart Dulles airport in Washington, and 8 hours later be in the main railway station in Frankfurt having never been exposed to the elements. For those interested in more statistics: the airport employes more than 25,000 individuals and thus is one of the largest industries in the state of Hessen, its underground garage has space for 6,000 automobiles, and as the home base for the German Lufthansa airline the airport boasts the largest maintenance hangar in the world, capable of holding 6 jumbo jets at one time. For those not interested in statistics, please ignore the above.

The Cathedral
(number 1 on map)

The cathedral was built from 1315 — 1410, and through the centuries was the electoral church and coronation cathedral of the German emperors. Its tower was rebuilt in the 1870s according to the original plans, after the fire of 1867 destroyed the temporary cupola which had been in place since the 14th century. The cathedral contains several medieval altars and the tomb of Guenther von Schwarzburg. He was proclamed King in January 1349 and died in June 1349.

The Arts and Crafts Museum

The Arts and Crafts Museum is located in Sachsenhausen at the end of the Eiserner Steg, just across the Main from the Roemer at Schaumainkai 15. It displays a cross-section of porcelaine, furniture and handicrafts of all periods and all peoples. — Open: Tuesday through Sunday: 10-17 hours; Wednesday: 10-20 hours.

City Hall, Roëmer and Kaisersaal   (number 2 on map)

Frankfurt's noted landmark, the five-gabled front facing Roemerberg square, is now once again seat of the city administration. Originally the private home of a wealthy merchant, the Roemer was purchased by the town council in 1405 for use as a town hall. In succeeding centuries, the neighboring dwellings were also bought up and joined to the Roemer where in the Middle Ages traders from Rome displayed their wares during the annual fairs. The upper floor of the Roemer is taken up almost entirely by the Imperial Hall—the Kaisersaal. Here crowned sovereigns of the Holy Roman Realm held their coronation banquets from 1562 to the end of the Empire in 1806. Today, the emperor's staircase is ascended daily by young Frankfurt couples on their way to the city registrar's office where civil marriage ceremonies are performed. Guided tours of the historic building group including Kaisersaal and adjoining courts and staircases are conducted daily 9-18 hours, and Sundays and holidays 10-16 hours.

Eschenheimer Tower

(number 9 on map)

The only surviving remnant of the city's inner fortification belt, the Eschenheimer Tower dates back to the Middle Ages. Built in 1426, the tower was occupied until 1957 when its last keeper, 77 year old hermit Johann Geiger died in his sleep.

International Fair Grounds

(number 21 on map)

Hardly a week passes without a major event or exhibit scheduled on the 90 acre site near the main railway station. High points are the annual spring and fall fairs, a tradition since the 14th century. The fairgrounds currently comprise 16 exhibit halls and 10 permanent foreign pavilions in addition to the indoor arena seating

The court of imperial Germany headed by Emperor William II appears in Roman togas to lay the cornerstone of the reconstructed Roman fortress Saalburg near Bad Homburg, 1899.

King Umberto of Italy strides past the Hauptbahnhof on a visit in 1889.

Frankfurt Hauptbahnhof painted by Max Beckmann in his exile 1942.

Ice floes on the Main as they appeared to painter Max Beckmann, 1923.

7,000 used for races, ice shows, pop concerts and sports competitions.

The Federal Postal Museum

Reflecting Frankfurt's position of significance as a vital crossroads of postal traffic, the Federal Postal Museum displays its collections of valuable material from the history of post and communication from all over the world. Special exhibits with collections of special themes are held regularly.— Open: Tuesday through Sunday: 10-17 hours; Wednesday: 10-20 hours.

Goethe House   (number 3 on map)

Birthplace of Germany's most famous poet and playwright, Johann Wolfgang von Goethe (1749-1832). Destroyed during the war, the literary shrine was rebuilt from the ground up in 1947, according to the original designs. Each building stone, girder or window frame that could be found beneath the rubble was put back into place and the new components fashioned with painstaking care into exact replicas of the old. The original furniture, books and documents of the poet's family, evacuated for safe keeping, were all in place when the Goethe House re-opened to the public in an impressive ceremony, attended by the President of Germany, Professor Theodor Heuss in May 1951. Since that time, millions of visitors from around the world have crossed the threshold of the home where the prodigious author of Faust, Werther, and many of the other great works of world literature spent his untroubled childhood. Germany's cultural center in New York, the 'Goethe House' of the new world opened in spring 1957, is named likewise in honor of the Frankfurt genius. Goethe's birthplace on Grosser Hirschgraben 23 and the adjoining museum are open daily from 9-18 hours; Sunday 10-13 hours.

Hauptwache

The Hauptwache was built in 1729 as the guard-house for the Frankfurt militia and was essentially a police station of the times. It also served as a prison. In the course of its history it was the focal point of numerous riots and rebellions, including the famous uprising of 1833. The Hauptwache was dismanteled and rebuilt brick-by-brick in 1968 in order to make room for the subway station that bears its name. It now contains a coffee house, and the "B-level" of the subway station adjacent to it, has become the most popular rendezvous point in the city.

Historical Museum   (number 7 on map)

The historical museum is the repository of the city's art treasures, historical documents, etchings, period furniture, silver and porcelain of Frankfurt manufactures. The museum which had previously consisted of several buildings, since 1972 has been housed in a new building complex across from the Roemer. This building incorporates the Saalhofkapelle, which as the 12th century chapel of Em-

peror Barbarossa is the oldest building left standing in Frankfurt. The entire structure is an interesting combination of Frankfurt architecture from the oldest to the newest. Treasures of the museum range from Duerer altars to a ceremonial vessel presented as a token of gratitude for the tolerant treatment of English protestant refugees in 1559.

Unusual exhibits include a coin collection and an exhibit of toys. The museum is recognized for its modern presentations and its attempts not only to display its treasures, but also to explain their significance through use of films, slides and recordings, and for introducing children to museums in the so-called children's museum. The museum is also host to jazz concerts, lectures and classic movies. — Visiting hours: Tuesday through Sunday: 10-17 hours; Wednesday: 10-20 hours.

I. G. Farben Building (Abrams Building)   (number 25 on map)

Formerly site of the globe-girdling chemicals concern, the building was completed in 1928 and for a long time ranked as Germany's largest office structure. General

Eisenhower had his offices here as SHAEF and USFET commander in 1945, and it was in the I. G. Farben building that he met President Truman during the Potsdam Conference. Now owned by the German Federal Government, the structure currently houses the headquarters of the Fifth U. S. Army Corps with affiliated units. In April 1975 the building was renamed the Creighton W. Abrams Building by the U. S. Army in honor of the late Army Chief of Staff who had served as Commander of Fifth Corps in this building from 1963 to 1964.

Iron Footbridge (Eiserner Steg)

Built in 1868, the Iron Footbridge connects Frankfurt with Sachsenhausen, its suburb across the Main. At its base on the Frankfurt side, sightseeing boats offer the visitor an opportunity to see the panorama of Frankfurt from the river. Every Saturday morning hundreds of Frankfurters cross to the other side to buy antiques and junk at the Sachsenhausen Flea Market.

Municipal Museum of Sculptures (number 12 on map)

Known as the Liebieg House after the baron who initially owned the riverside mansion acquired by the city in 1909, the museum effectively displays sculptures of all periods in its rooms and spacious garden. Notable examples of Egyptian, Greek and Roman plastic arts vie for attention in the drapery-lined rooms along with German, French and Flemish sculptures of the renaissance and modern period. Myron's 'Athena', a life-size statue dating back to classical Greece of the 5th century B. C. is perhaps the most important piece in the collection, the most unusual and amusing is the statuette of a Sumerian bureaucrat, more than 4000 years old. Limited space in the museum unfortunately prevents the display of more than a fraction of the 1200 sculptures in the collection and the weather conditions do not exactly favor extended outdoor exhibit of the most precious pieces. However, the items displayed, some of which were originally obtained by Frankfurt explorer Dr. Eduard Rueppell during his African travels in the 1820s are well worth seeing. Open Tuesday through Sunday 10-17 hours, Wednesdays 10-20 hours.

Opera and Theater (number 17 on map)

Frankfurt's wealthier citizens have always been proud of the fact that they patronize the arts, especially the theater. By the turn of the century, Frankfurt's theater had become world-famous. However, during the last war, the many theater buildings were wiped out, and performances were possible in the early post war years only in the stock exchange, and in a few other small auditoriums. The inauguration of the new theater complex in 1963, hosting three theaters under one roof — the opera, the playhouse, and an experimental theater — was an accomplishment of the first order. The new building met all the requirements of modern theater and provided a proper setting for artists like world-famous conductors George Solti and Christoph v. Dohnanyi, whose performances of Mozart and Wagner, as well as modern composers such as Schoenberg and Hindemith gained world-wide recognition. Director Harry Buckwitz became most famous for his Bert Brecht stagings at the playhouse. American playwright Thornton Wilder maintained a close connection with the Frankfurt playhouse, and his "Alcestiade" had its world premier there. The Frankfurt ballet became famous under the direction of John Neumeier, gifted student of John Cranko. In the lobby of the building hang a series of paintings entitled "Comedia dell'arte" by Marc Chagall. Besides the municipal theater, several smaller theaters vie for the attention of the Frankfurt theatergoer.

The Old Opera House

The ruins of the old Opera House on Opernplatz are one of the city's most impressive sights. Built in 1880 as a replica of the Paris opera, the lavish interior caused Emperor William to remark caustically: "Only the city of Frankfurt could afford such splendor", as he ascended the marble staircase for the premiere performance. Almost every famous opera star sang here between 1880 and 1944, the year the building was destroyed by bombs. Ever since the end of the war, Frankfurt's citizens have dreamed of the time that the old Opera House would be rebuilt. Finally, in 1964 the president of the Frankfurt Chamber of Commerce and Industry, Dr. Fritz Dietz, became the chairman of the committee for the reconstruction of the old Opera House. Since then gifts from private individuals and organizations, subsidized by the city, have brought the dream closer to reality. Construction is finally under way to restore the building as a concert and convention hall, hopefully in time for its 100th anniversary in 1980.

Palm Garden   (number 15 on map)

Plants and trees from all five continents line the zig-zag route of an afternoon stroll through the green-houses of this botanical garden. A bandstand offering afternoon and evening concerts during the summer, a restaurant and a spacious park complete the picture.

Paul's Church   (number 19 on map)

Seat of the first popularly-elected German parliament in 1848, this secularized church has become a symbol of German unification and democracy. It currently serves as an assembly and exhibit hall, is built of red sandstone, took forty years to complete and possesses some most unusual acoustics. President Kennedy delivered an address here in 1963. A plaque commemorating his visit is affixed to the outside wall of the church.

Johann Friedrich Staedel, described by Goethe as 'the dean of the art patrons living here' left his collection of 450 oil paintings and nearly a million dollars to the art foundation set up by his will when he died in 1816. Administered by a board of trustees, far-sightedly given wide discretion over the art purchases of the private foundation, the Staedel Institute has accumulated notable canvasses of every school and period. A palace-like structure it was built late in the last century to house the growing collection, and a new wing was added after 1910. Today, the rambling building on the south bank of the Main is filled to the eaves with works by such masters as Botticelli, Canaletto, Duerer, Holbein, Goya, Rembrandt, van Eyck and the 19th century immortals Cezanne, Corot, Courbet, Degas, Delacroix, Manet, Monet and van Gogh. The museum has restored its collection of canvasses confiscated by the Nazis as 'degenerate art' and largely disposed of abroad for hard currencies during the Hitler period. One of the painters whose works were affected by this move was Max Beckmann, adopted Frankfurter and outstanding modern artist. His representative paintings are now on view at the Museum of Modern Art in New York, where he spent the last years of his life. The painter lived in Frankfurt from 1917-1933 and taught for part of that period at the Staedel Art School, associated with the institute. The museum recently acquired his painting of the Frankfurt Synagogue with money raised from the public sale of poster copies of the painting. The Staedel is also noted for its collection of copper engravings, including drawings of Titian, Tintoretto, Raphael among the Italians; Rembrandt, Breughel, Rubens, van Dyck among the Dutch; and with Fragonard, Boucher and Watteau representing the French. — Open: Tuesday through Sunday: 10-17 hours; Wednesday: 10-20 hours.

St. Leonhard Church (number 6 on map)

Started in the 13th century, St. Leonhard's is specially noted for its romanesque portal and the 'hanging vault', considered a masterwork of late gothic masonry. Journeymen masons were expected to pass by the city and inspect this marvel of the craft, to complete their education, according to the travel lore reported in guide books of the 18th century. A noted altar painting by Hans Holbein graces the interior of the church, built on property presented 'for the sake of my immortal soul' to the citizens of Frankfurt by Emperor Frederick II in 1219. The donation parchment bearing the imperial seal is preserved to this day in the city's archives.

Museum of Archeology

(number 13 on map)

Traces left by the stone age inhabitants of the Rhein Main area are on view here, together with trinkets left behind by Roman settlers in their hurried departure before invading tribes in the third century. In digging the foundations of modern office and buildings on the site of the old city, construction workers found the remnants of Roman baths interspersed with the walls of the original palace built by the Carolingian kings in the 9th century. Finds from the Roman suburb of Nida, now Heddernheim, and from a small border fortress on the site of the present cathedral are also included in the collection, tracing life in Frankfurt back to the stone flints and war axes of the third millenium B. C. The museum is located on Justinianstrasse 5 and is open Tuesdays through Sundays 10-17 hours, Wednesday 10-20 hours.

St. Nikolai Church

(number 5 on map)

Dedicated to the patron saint of fishermen in gratitude for the city's successful weathering of destructive floods, St. Nikolai is first mentioned in 1246. The characteristic gallery at the edge of the roof used by city councillors and the town's well-connected families as a vantage point to watch festivities including coronation proceedings in the square below, was added in the 15th century. It became Frankfurt's first protestant church and the official house of worship for the city government. Before each session of the town council, councilmen would come in a body to attend services while the bells of St. Nikolai tolled for half an hour. Bleached skulls of oxen, sarcastically referred to as 'the only relics of the Holy Roman Empire' used to hang on the outside walls of St. Nikolai in the early 19th century as a reminder of the recurring coronation festivities on Roemerberg square. During the fairs also, the church was surrounded by much worldly activity. A tightrope walker from Venice, reports the 1543 fair chronicle, displayed his skills on a cable stretched taut from the spire of St. Nikolai to the salt house at the edge of the square below. Nowaday the choraleers of St. Nikolai stand on the roof to sing Christmas carols to the crowds during the holiday season while the Christmas market is in full swing on the Roemerberg. The traditional carillon has been re-installed in the spire of St. Nikolai, in place of the town crier who used to sound his bugle from atop the lookout point to announce the arrival and departure of vessels with the hymnal tune "In God's Name We Sail."

Race Track   (number 19 on map)

Flat and steeplechase racing throughout the summer season. Record pari-mutual payoff here was in 1911 when long shot 'Baro' returned 2924 Marks for 10. Forest stadium near racetrack seats 90,000, has adjoining swimming pool, tennis and race courses including an arena for track and field events. The extensive sports area is located off Moerfelder Landstraße.

Sports Stadium (number 18 on map)

A good highway, trains and buses enable visitors to reach the sports center with its varied facilities in less than ten minutes from the heart of the city. Besides the main stadium holding 62,000, the center includes a large gym, a swimming pool, bicycle race courses, indoor ice rink and tennis courts. The whole sports area lies embedded in the municipal forest — once Charlemagne's private hunting preserve — on the southern edge of the city. The Stadion has seen such diversified events as the Cassius Clay versus Karl Mildenberger heavyweight championship fight, a Billy Graham campaign and the 1974 World Cup Soccer Matches. In addition, the center of the sports area is the home of the Federal Sports School.

Telephone and Telegraph Building (number 10 on map)

Juxtaposed with the 500 year-old Eschenheimer tower, the glass and steel telephone tower of the Federal Post Office hase become the architectural symbol of the new Frankfurt. Every long distance call of the 1.6 million subscribers in the district, extending from Fulda in the North to Kaiserslautern in the south, clears through relays in the Frankfurt exchange. International radio, telephone and telegraph lines, lately also Germany's coaxial television cables meet and intersect in the basement of the 16-story building where some 4,000 employees process over 1,7 million electrically-transmitted messages daily. And daily, over 50,000 direct connections are set up to and from 65 other countries: Brazil calls Israel via Frankfurt; Kuwait likewise contacts Venezuela via Frankfurt.

The eighth floor houses 120 teletype machines in a single spacious hall, comprising a major division of the European cable and telex net. The telephone exchange occupies the site of the old Thurn and Taxis palace, destroyed in the war. The baroque palace doorway which led to the residence of the princes, franchised to operate the postal system of the Empire as a private venture, now opens appropriately enough unto the district headquarters of the German Fedreal Post Office, completed in 1956.

Planned for completion in 1978 is the telecommunication tower under construction in the suburb of Ginnheim. It will be 331 meters high — over 1,000 feet, and house the most modern relay equipment and microwave antennas.

Stock Exchange   (number 8 on map)

Linked historically with the markets of the United States and other 'exotics' as the debentures of overseas territories used to be called in the 'good old days', before the advent of the telephone and the transatlantic cable, the reconstructed Frankfurt Exchange is actively trading in American securities. By tradition and volume, Frankfurt counts among the oldest and largest stock and commodity exchanges on the European continent. Even before 1800, foreign securities were traded here by financial wizards like Rothschild and Bethmann who financed whole countries in credit transactions. And this at a time when exchange activities were limited to business hours running from noon to 1 o'clock on Tuesdays and Fridays. The present stock exchange building, erected in 1879 and restored in 1957 after war-time damage, is a major landmark of the city.

Wholesale Market

(number 23 on map)

At the time of their construction in 1929, the wholesale market halls of Frankfurt were considered the largest and best-equipped in this part of Europe. Their height and seize soon earned them the nickname: 'vegetable church'. Shortly after they opened for business, the hall's unusual acoustics were put to the test by tens of thousands of amateur singers who convened here for a giant songfest in 1932. The place is busiest just before dawn when food supplies from the countryside are broken down among the food chains and retailers to feed the 700,000 maws of the metropolis.

University

(number 14 on map)

The Johann Wolfgang Goethe University founded at Frankfurt in 1914 is one of the younger institutions of higher learning in Germany. It is distinguished from its older confreres not only by relative youth but by the condition of its birth as a brainchild of businessmen rather than princes. Known for its faculty of social studies, many of whose members went into exile during the Nazi dictatorship, Frankfurt University was able to emerge from the period of thought control relatively unharmed when its noted educators returned from their teaching positions abroad. Sociology professors Theodor Adorno, Max Horkheimer, who taught at Columbia, and several of their colleagues managed to keep up their research and publications during the emigration period. Contacts dating from that time brought about such useful arrangements as exchange professorships and coordinated research programs between the universities of Frankfurt and Chicago. Frankfurt's student body is growing steadily each year and currently comprises some 22,000 young men and women from all parts of Germany.

The Senckenberg Natural History Museum

The Senckenberg Natural History Museum, located in the heart of the university area, carries the name of the Frankfurt doctor whose donations late in the eighteenth century gave the impetus to local scientific research culminating in the founding of the university. Outstanding in its field, the museum includes a fine collection of fossils, headed by a 72 foot dinosaur, gift of the New York Museum of Natural History. The museum is opened daily from 9-16 hours, on Wednesdays, Fridays and Sundays: 9-20 hours.

The Senckenberg Natural History Research Society was founded in 1817 at the suggestion of Johann Wolfgang Goethe to create a "Nature Museum". In the first half of the last century the Senckenberg-Museum joined the rank of world museums through the exploratory expeditions and scientific activities of Eduard Rüppell. Today the Senckenberg is the largest research museum in Germany and one of the most important museums of the world. Its research departments and areas of study are zoology, botany, geology, paleontology, marine biology as well as marine geology, ecology, and anthropology. The Senckenberg Natural History Research Society is a free and independent establishment. Both the museum and the research departments with their scientific collections are owned by this society.

The Zoo

(number 16 on map)

The name Prof. Bernhard Grzimek is synonymous with the Frankfurt Zoo. And well it should be for without his efforts, the Frankfurt Zoo probably would not exist today. During World War II, the existing Frankfurt Zoo was badly damaged, and at war's end only 10 animals survived. Because of its sorry state, many city officials were in favor of closing the Zoo completely, and putting rebuilding priorities elsewhere. But the acting police president of Frankfurt, a relatively unknown refugee from Berlin, Bernhard Grzimek, plead the case for the Frankfurt Zoo so persuasively that he was relieved of his duties as police chief and given the job of rebuilding the Zoo. Under his dynamic leadership the Frankfurt Zoo has become world-famous.

Prof. Grzimek has led several expeditions to Africa. He has written numerous books and his "Serengeti Shall Not Die" has been translated into English as well as many other languages. He retired as director of the Zoo in 1974, but is still active in the cause of wildlife preservation.

Part of the Zoo's success comes from the innovative advertising used. At almost every bus and subway stop in Frankfurt one sees a poster advertising the current attraction at the Zoo.

The Zoo boasts an Exotarium which presents fish, birds and reptiles in a native habitat, an animal nursery and a monkey-house, which are favorites of children, and an aviary, which includes a tropical rain forest, among others. The Zoo is famous for many "first births in captivity", including the first gorilla born in captivity in 1965.

The Zoo is still at its original location, occupying a plot of land only 30 acres in size, within walking distance of the middle of the city. As it is completely surrounded by houses and businesses, there is no chance for expansion at this location. Fortunately, 175 acres of land are available in Ginnheim at the northwest edge of Frankfurt and the Zoo plans to move some of its larger exhibits to the "Nidda-Zoo" in the near future.

In the more immediate future the Grzimek-Haus will be opened as the "24-hour-house". Modeled after the "World of Darkness" in New York, and by controlling light and temperature, night and day will be reversed for the nocturnal animals on display, so that the visitor will be able to observe the animals' natural nighttime behaviour.

THE FEMININE SIDE

In outward appearance, Frankfurt has always been a man's world, a world of businessmen. But the great clans of merchants, the family of families that set the city's pace, were in turn run quietly and efficiently over the generations by countless mothers, grandmothers and great grandmothers. Family life gravitated around the matriarch and inroads into the business community by the arts, music and literature were made largely through the feminine side of the household. Like a state within a state, cutting across political and economic boundaries, the Frankfurt family group radiated in all directions.

Sons of merchants and traders founded families as well as branch offices in other cities. The lines of commerce stretched into many countries. But as they went forth into the world, the patricians of old Frankfurt would return on extended visits to the family circle, bringing wives, children and grandchildren to meet the determined old ladies who ran their far-flung household in dowager fashion. Their world was the family, and inside the family, the finer things of life had their duly appointed place. Musical evenings, art and literary circles as an adjunct of costly private collections, and an elaborate sociability prevailed in the town houses of the wealthy. There were the so-called 'sweet evenings', with cakes, tea and dancing and the 'card game with bread and butter evenings', a modest name covering banquets with the choicest of wines. Over the manifold social events, the matrons presided. Their advice was sought and respected in family councils on matters of marriage, the upbringing of children and the major decisions in the lives of the younger generation.

When the occasion demanded, they would even leave their traditional surroundings and carry on the family business in place of their husbands. An outstanding example was the pretty Johanna Rosina Scheel who took over her husband's interior decorating establishment on his death and made it the most successful in the city early in the last century. She left her family a sizeable fortune and a famous art collection. Christina Barbara Metzler managed her husband's banking firm maintaining its sound position for a generation after his death in 1757.

Due to Frankfurt's position astride the commerce lanes of Europe, wives and daughters of the leading citizens traditionally followed the latest fashion dictates. The fairs brought Italian silks and brocades, Belgian lace and jewelry to the city, and even the maids and servants of the patrician traders had a reputation for costly dress and independent mannerisms. In later years, particularly in the Napoleonic era, the French influence in fashion came to the fore in the city frequently occupied by French troops and allied with France under a Grand Duke installed by Napoleon.

The way of life enjoyed by Frankfurt's upper classes, however, was not always as staid and steadfast as the studied portrait poses would make us assume. Particularly in the ribald Middle Ages, military campaigns, councils, imperial coronations and the flow of trade brought to the city adventurous foreigners, courtesans, camp followers and a style of living that proved an eyesore to the core of sober and self-righteous citizens.

In 1411, Emperor Sigismund and his courtiers were entertained at city expense by medieval call girls employed municipally in houses specially set aside for that purpose. A general decline of morals also set in among propertied, upper-class citizens during that period. Councillors would draw knives on each other in open session, and blasphemy, lewdness and corruption ran rampant, in the words of Luther who stopped here in 1521, even among those in authority. Puritans were outraged that the sexes bathed together in public steam baths attended by loosely-clad women attendants, and that it was considered a prime rule of courtesy to conduct dinner guests to the public baths after they had enjoyed patrician hospitality.

The public nuisance wrought by out-of-town nobles attending the imperial assemblies called together periodically in the city reached such proportions that the city council issued a formal edict warning citizens to keep their wives and daughters indoors after sundown to avoid molestation and the unseemly sight of lewd carousing on the streets of Frankfurt.

Local women of ill repute were reinforced during the fairs and coronations by camp followers from distant cities. A chronicler meticulously recorded the presence of 800 camp followers within the city limits on the occasion of the imperial conclave of 1394.

The exclusive clan-like Alt-Limpurg Society which united the wealthiest old families and kept a strict eye on the manners and morals of members, worried a great

Patrician citizens of Frankfurt on their way to a dance.
(Doodle of a city clerk, 1405.)

deal about exposure of its younger generation to the
sight of the vices and loose behavior encountered in cosmopolitan Frankfurt. In the dances organized by the
Society, young gentlemen were strictly enjoined against
encircling the waist of their partner and introducing
uncouth, wild dances in place of the prescribed measured
gait called for by custom and the complicated feminine
fashions of the period with their high peaked caps and
long wide trains.

Apprentices and farmers' daughters meanwhile amused
themselves in the wild dance frowned upon by the city
fathers. Perhaps an early forerunner of 'rock n' roll', the
'moorish dance' (*Moriskentanz*) was attributed to Berber

tribesmen who brought it to Spain under Arab rule. It was characterized by the wailing of bagpipes, excessive contortions, wild shouts and the occasional painting of face and limbs, a practice soon outlawed by the city council.

The deep social divisions even among the commoners of the free city, sanctioned varied codes of conduct among the different classes. A modified caste system, written into law in 1621, provided for five classes of citizens along a descending scale of dress and privilege. A move from class to class by marriage or by achievement was possible, but rare, and it is said that the desire of society ladies to protect by law the exclusive elegance of their garments from imitation by rich upstarts was a motivating force of the new legislation. The first of the five classes was formed by the judges and landed old family clans—about a dozen of them—organized as a sort of exclusive club in the Alt Limpurg Society; the second group united all city councillors and councilmen; the third included distinguished tradesmen, notaries and business managers; in the fourth group could be found common merchants and artisans and finally in the fifth the lowest class of laborers, coachmen and teamsters. A 'Morals Commission' watched over observance of the clothing and luxury regulations. A century later, according to the 'Luxury Laws' of 1731, members of the first class, enlarged over the years to include doctors and most city officials, were permitted to wear all sorts of silks, brocaded vests, gold or silver-trimmed collars and to carry gold, though not jewelled watches. Members of the second group, also enlarged to include officers of the civil militia and property owners with holdings in excess of 20,000 dollars could dress themselves in embroidered white vests and carry silver watches. Though they were allowed all manners of silks and textiles they were enjoined against gold and silver trimmings, velvet lining and sashes. The third class had to confine themselves to solid colors in their garments, wives and daughters had to wear plain coats without flaps; the fourth had to do without wigs and the lowest class was allowed no jewelry of any kind and but the plainest of shoes. The worth of the dowry was minutely prescribed for each class running from the equivalent of 1000 dollars down to 20; and there were first, second, third, fourth and fifth class funerals. Unkind souls maintain that frills in the fifth-class funeral were cut practically to the point where the deceased had to reach the cemetery on foot, carrying a candle.

Many an early demise among the wealthy classes was caused by overeating. Festive banquets running to ten or more courses were the rule rather than an exception in medieval Frankfurt and the amounts consumed at a single sitting are staggering to the modern mind. The same luxury control laws that prescribed dress and entertainment styles for the various classes, limited meals to eight courses. But the tradition of elaborate eating remained unaffected through the years, lending endless inspiration to the first German still life painter, Georg Flegel, whose productive years appropriately enough, were spent in this city.

Tempted by the ample dishes of Frankfurt housewives, described as a mixture of the North and South German

A dowager of 16th century Frankfurt drawn in her stately robes by Jost Amman, 1586.

with a dash of French, local society down to this century remained sublimely unconcerned with the medical effects of too much food. Only the deprivations faced in recent decades has brought home the fact that people can get along on much less food than previously supposed. A traveler of the Victorian age still had this to say about dinners prepared for the tourist at the better hotels: "in stepping up to a Frankfurt table one might believe that the chefs here are working for a special nation of heavy eaters: beef follows the soup, side dishes follow the beef; ragouts of all kinds are joined by puddings; fish follows the pudding and roasts are tacked on to the fish. Thus it continues up to the dessert. It seems that a whole army is deployed atop the table, and eating your way through becomes devilish work indeed. That's why doctors are the busiest people in Frankfurt, and cooks here draw higher wages than authors."

A spate of Frankfurt cooking specialties developed as a result of the interest taken in the delights of the table. In many cases, housewives interpreted and varied the standard French sauces, coming up with an endless variety of the local 'chü' (adaptation of the French 'jus'), but a few characteristic garnishings defy a definition of origin.

Outstanding as a local specialty is the so-called green sauce ('gruene Sosse'), taken with fish and meats: Here is the recipe: Go into any Frankfurt grocery in the spring and ask for 'gruene Sosse'. You'll get a package of herbs; they're relatively outlandish like *Boretsch, Pimpernell* and *Drachant,* but chop them up fine and mix them with the yellow of three hardboiled eggs mashed together with one and a half tablespoons of olive oil, a tablespoon of vinegar and half a teaspoon of mustard. Add three tablespoons of sour cream and press the mixture through a fine sieve. Opinions vary greatly on Frankfurt's green sauce. Some find it vile, other delightful. There are no neutrals.

Green sauce is only one of a wide range of accomplishments by Frankfurt's fair sex. In the poetic regions a whole bevy of late eighteenth-century lovelies was immortalized by Johann Wolfgang von Goethe, the nation's greatest playwright who was born and bred in the city more than 200 years ago. His romantic attachments in these parts, notably the passion conceived by the 66 year old Goethe for Marianne von Willemer, wife of a local banker, produced some of the greatest poetry in the German language.

Frau Rat Goethe, the poet's mother, who spent her whole life in Frankfurt and is buried there, was a wise and wide-awake correspondent in her own right. Her letters to her famous son at the court of Weimar mirror the manners and morals of middle class life in the declining years of the city state.

Women of Frankfurt, courageous and kind in their ways, often furnished the color and backbone to a history left predominantly gray by a policy of self-protection practiced timidly by their husbands. Aged Anna von Holzhausen had herself carried to the inn where Martin Luther stopped en route to the Diet of Worms in 1521 to kiss the hands of the religious reformer and offer him a welcome goblet of malmsey at a time his own fate and that of his supporters hung in the balance. More than three centuries later, Marianne Lutteroth's candid protests shamed Prussian chancellor Otto von Bismarck into lightening the occupation burden and ending the excesses of Prussian troops and military government authorities in the annexed city.

In the arts particularly, women of Frankfurt excelled. Sybilla Merian, daughter of the noted painter and engraver, brought the art of painting birds, butterflies and flowers from nature to a heretofore unknown state of perfection. Blessed by talent rather than good looks, adventurous Sybilla traveled to Surinam in 1698, at a time when a trip to Mainz or Wiesbaden demanded a measure of daring and nonchalance from a single woman. Commissioned by the Netherlands government, Sybilla Merian drew and engraved an unequalled collection of color plates giving Europe its first glance at the strange metamorphosis of caterpillars, insect life and butterflies in the West Indies. Unaffected by the passage of time, the painstaking water colors and engravings of the woman who went forth into the jungle, equipped only with canvas and easel are on view at the Staedel Art Institute. *"Sybille a Surinam va chercher la nature: Elle affronte les vents, elle brave les flots: Avec l'esprit d'un sage et le coeur d'un heros"* was the eulogy of a French poet when the pioneer of the arts died in 1717 at the age of 70.

Other Frankfurt girls made their mark as portrait and landscape painters, among them Maria Eleonora Hochecker, Margaretha Elisabeth Soemmering, wife of the physician who invented the electric telegraph, and Maria Katharina Prestel, whose aquatint paintings were known throughout Europe in the early nineteenth century.

The belles of upper-class Frankfurt also furnished the subject of many a noted portrait in the romantic period, among them the canvas of Anna, Karoline and Julia Schwendler, daughters of the first U. S. Consul in Germany who established and ran the Frankfurt Consulate from 1829 until his death in 1853. Two of the daughters married Frankfurt citizens and their descendants remain active in the city's business life to this day.

A modern development of the graphic arts — fashion design — is now winning new converts annually among the students attending the three year course at the city-sponsored fashion institute. Most of the prospective dress designers, are girls, and their effect on the fashion-consciousness of Frankfurt, a trait perhaps more evident in the old days, will provide a subject for debate by future historians.

'Rothschild Love Dollar', the last coin struck by the Free City in 1866, reputed to show actress Fanny Janauschek, one of the financial wizard's romantic attachments, as a symbolic 'Francofurtia'.

BARON ROTHSCHILD'S LOVE DOLLARS

Once upon a time there was a beautiful actress, christened Franziska Magdalena Romance. Even though she relinquished this name in favor of a modest 'Fanny Janauschek', she reaped artistic triumph after triumph in the Frankfurt of a hundred years ago. About that time the city's own mint struck a one taler coin showing a symbolic female 'Francofurtia', whose features were said to resemble the famous actress far closer than a coincidence could account for. The sculptor who designed the coin vehemently denied the connection, but immediately the rumor got started that the city was using the face of Baron Rothschild's girlfriend on its new talers to flatter the head of the financial dynasty. The rumor didn't exactly get squelched when Fanny Janauschek appeared as 'Francofurtia' at various patriotic festivities.

Though the facts never bore out that Fanny modeled for the city mint, the coin, the resemblance, and the Rothschild girlfriend theory made a good story and 'Rothschild Love Dollars', as they began to be called, obtained a ready market as collectors' items in many countries, including the United States. There are still a few around in Frankfurt, worked mainly into candy trays, cigaret boxes and other souvenirs. Jeweler Hessenberg appears to have cornered the local market on this item:

The Janauschek story unfortunately lacked a happy ending as the actress died destitute in New York in 1904.

She broke with the Frankfurt theater in 1860, spent some years in Munich where King Ludwig, known for his infatuations, is said to have attended 36 of her performances in a row, presenting her each time with a hyacinth, her favorite flower. She then toured the U. S. as a phenomenally successful 'Medea' in 1867. During a seven month series of theatrical engagements, Fanny earned a record sum of 95,000 dollar, at a time when a steak dinner cost 25 cents. But high living and bad investments claimed most of her earnings and she was said to be penniless when she died at the age of 74.

The city mint she made famous beyond the borders of Germany struck its last coin when Frankfurt lost its independent status and became part of Prussia in 1866. Before that time, the mint turned out a variety of imperial and local coins including the highly-prized coronation medals. Some 12,000 local specimens, dating back to the first coinage of 1160 are preserved in the Historical Museum comprising one of the largest collections in Germany. During recent excavations on the site of the old city, additional old coins minted around 1320 were unearthed and now form part of the collection.

THE AEPPELWOI

I have yet to find a foreigner who liked Aeppelwoi, the sour cider that is Frankfurt's national beverage. But it's a conditioned taste like Martinis, perhaps even more so, and many modern Frankfurters haven't been properly conditioned either.

Aeppelwoi is traditionally served in a characteristic fat-bellied dispenser of blue glazed stoneware, known affectionately as a 'Bembel'. Most of the inns specializing

Conviviality and apple wine in Sachsenhausen (pen and ink drawing by Lino Salini, 1913).

in the brew have now moved across the river to Sachsen-hausen, where the necessary atmosphere still prevails among the narrow, crooked lanes with its shingled, off-center buildings in a rustic setting. The inns are marked with a pine bough dangling from a pole over the entrance and their patrons take liquid nourishment seated on benches around long wooden tables. Since they (the inns, that is) are not too easy to find, particularly if one is looking for them, instead of stumbling upon them accidentally, they have retained a little of the unspoiled charm that usually eludes the tourist. Frankfurt artists feel the same way about it and have been draining their jugs for years in Aeppelwoi inns like the "Klaane Sachsehaeuser", "Fichte-kraenzi" and "Atschel".

The suburb of Heddernheim, built on the site of a Roman settlement also boasts cider bistros with plenty of local color. For residents there is the added attraction of puttering around in their gardens and coming up with Roman coins, pottery fragments and other remnants of the occupation two thousand years ago by the Fourteenth Roman Legion. Street signs reading Tiberius, Hadrian, Antoninus, Augustus, Severius and Domitianstrasse likewise are reminders of the original Roman empire that didn't even claim to be holy, and a newspaper friend of ours who lives on Augustusstrasse, displays on his mantelpiece a whole collection of Roman oil lamps his German shepherd dug out of the garden.

As we were speaking of Aeppelwoi before, this might be a good place to note that the first recorded mention of this beverage occurred a few hundred years after the Romans left. This does not mean that the Fourteenth

144

Germany's giant pre-war dirigibles a the home mooring on Frankfurt's Rhein Main airport. Photo taken in 1937 shows the 'Hindenburg' a few weeks before her tragic end at Lakehurst, New Jersey. Floating above, the 'Graf Zeppelin'.

'Three charming Frankfurt maids'. This colored engraving in the city's Historical Museum gives proof that the French 'empire style' had taken over Frankfurt fashions by 1800.

Ernst Schwendler, first U. S. Consul in Frankfurt (1829-1853) had three
charming daughters shown here in a period painting by Ernst Hickmann,
1847. Their descendants live in the city to this day.

JOHN FITZGERALD KENNEDY PRÄSIDENT
DER VEREINIGTEN STAATEN VON AMERIKA
GEBOREN 29. MAI 1917
ERMORDET 22. NOVEMBER 1963
SPRACH AM 25. JUNI 1963 IN DER PAULSKIR-
CHE ZUM DEUTSCHEN VOLK UND ZUR WELT:
„NIEMAND SOLL VON DIESER UNSERER
ATLANTISCHEN GENERATION SAGEN, WIR
HÄTTEN IDEALE UND VISIONEN DER VER-
GANGENHEIT, ZIELSTREBEN UND ENTSCHLOS-
SENHEIT UNSEREN GEGNERN ÜBERLASSEN."

Kennedy bas-relief at Paul's Church commemorating his speach
on 25 June 1963.

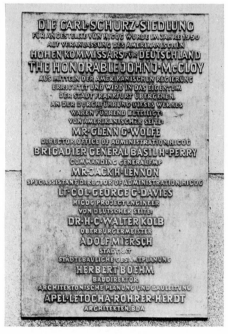

DIE CARL-SCHURZ-SIEDLUNG
FÜR ANGESTELLTE VON HICOG WURDE IM JAHRE 1950
AUF VERANLASSUNG DES AMERIKANISCHEN
HOHEN KOMMISSARS FÜR DEUTSCHLAND
THE HONORABLE JOHN J. McCLOY
AUS MITTELN DER AMERIKANISCHEN REGIERUNG
ERRICHTET UND WIRD IN DAS EIGENTUM
DER STADT FRANKFURT ÜBERGEHEN.
AN DER DURCHFÜHRUNG DIESES WERKES
WAREN FÜHREND BETEILIGT:
VON AMERIKANISCHER SEITE:
MR. GLENN G. WOLFE
DIRECTOR OFFICE OF ADMINISTRATION HICOG
BRIGADIER GENERAL BASIL H. PERRY
COMMANDING GENERAL FMP
MR. JACK H. LENNON
SPEC. ASSISTANT DIRECTOR OF ADMINISTRATION HICOG
LT. COL. GEORGE G. DAVIES
HICOG PROJECT ENGINEER
VON DEUTSCHER SEITE:
DR. H. C. WALTER KOLB
OBERBÜRGERMEISTER
ADOLF MIERSCH
STADTRAT
STÄDTEBAULICHE GESAMTPLANUNG
HERBERT BOEHM
BAUDIREKTOR
ARCHITEKTONISCHE PLANUNG UND BAULEITUNG
APEL · LETOCHA · ROHRER · HERDT
ARCHITEKTEN BDA

Memorial plaque at Carl-Schurz Housing Area, constructed in 1950
for the American military and their families.

Open air butcher's stalls in old Frankfurt—birthplace of the "Frankfurter".

Legion didn't know how to make Aeppelwoi. They just didn't bother to inform posterity. But Ernst Weill from Pirmasens who made Frankfurter Aeppelwoi the subject of a doctoral thesis in 1928, discovered that Charlemagne authorized all of his provincial governors to include brewers of apple wine and beer on their staffs, as well as amorers, silversmiths and goldsmiths.

In the Middle Ages, Frankfurt citizens were known to have more wine in their cellars than water in their wells and some of the casks surely held liquid apples. Taxation first struck the Aeppelwoi in 1654 and considering that more than a quarter million gallons are consumed in Sachsenhausen annually, it has remained a good source of revenue ever since. It also provided Ernst Weill with a doctor's degree and over the centuries, millions of Frankfurters with their jug of enjoyment. And consider the billions of 'Frankfurters' washed down by these millions of Frankfurters. Which brings us to the fact that to most of the world, 'Frankfurter' calls up the image of 'a highly seasoned sausage' in the words of Webster, rather than a native of the ancient free city. In a sense, the globe-girdling Frankfurter has been the most effective good-will messenger ever dispatched by a community, and inadvertently at that.

Open-air butcher's stalls vending sausages are reported by chroniclers in old Frankfurt since the beginning of the 14th century. Hundreds of them clustered around the old market square were a major sight of pre-war Frankfurt. The stalls did not survive the war, but the Frankfurters now on sale throughout Germany in their new acetate jackets are as successful as ever, even in competition with the American 'Frankfurters', on sale in the local Army commissary. Around the turn of the century, incidentally, local sausages started to carry tags proclaiming *'echte Frankfurter Wuerstchen'* to distinguish them from the American Frankfurters, which, despite higher labor costs, are cheaper than those produced in the old home town. But the advent of deep freeze and automation in the sausage factory doesn't always improve the taste, and the genuine Frankfurt Frankfurter can feel safe in its limited but entirely tasteful edition.

FRANKFURT ANECDOTES

Anecdotes have a life of their own. They crop up in all parts of the world and are attributed in turn to the great men or the amusing also-rans typical of each age and civilization. There is probably no really new situation under the sun, but only an infinite number of variations for which anecdotes furnish the local flavor. Instances cited on the following pages are vouched for by old Frankfurters as having actually occured in this city. Be that as it may, the people to whom they are attributed stayed in Frankfurt and were characters. Who is to say they didn't happen?

Waldemar Kramer has published a whole collection of Frankfurt ancedotes from which some of the following were chosen. A wealth of local stories and amusing incidents, still more difficult to ferret out, are contained in the dialect writings of the local poet dynasty, Friedrich and Adolf Stoltze. The father and son team raised *'Frankforter Gebabbel un Gekrisch'* (literally, Frankfurt babblings and screechings) as the local dialect is sometimes referred to, to the status of a written language, giving humorous expression to the fierce but harmless local patriotism that is the trademark of the homegrown Frankfurter. Few foreigners —and that means anyone not baptized with Main water— are ever initiated into the mysteries of *'Frankforderisch'*. Why, will become apparent if you read, or rather try to read how Friedrich Stoltze feels about his native city, in a poem titled simply 'Frankfort'. The first verse along with its rather free translation is furnished here. The city built him a monument, unveiled in 1895, four years after his death. For purposes of comparison, Goethe's monument in Frankfurt was unveiled in 1844, twelve years after the death of that native son.

FRANKFORT

von Friedrich Stoltze (1816-1891)

Es is kaa Stadt uff der weite Welt,
die so merr wie mei Frankfort gefällt,
un es will merr net in mein Kopp enei:
wie kann nor e Mensch net von Frankfort sei!

There is no city in the whole wide world
That I like anymore than Frankfurt.
And it's impossible for me to comprehend
Anyone claiming any place else.

* * *

Violin virtuoso Nicoló Paganini (1782-1840) put his disordered financial affairs in the hands of a Frankfurt banker during one of his frequent concert appearances in this city. Knowing how some of his wealthy friends had exploited the good-natured though temperamental Italian by inviting him to private banquets ostensibly in his honor, at which he felt obliged to regale the guests with examples of his artistry free of charge, the banker let it be known that Paganini would not play in private homes under any circumstances. All the same, a successful whole-sale merchant invited the artist to a soiree at his palatial

148

residence, and himself went to pick up Paganini at the hotel. No sooner had the virtuoso seated himself in the trader's carriage, when his host said: 'But Maestro, you forgot your violin.' 'Stop the car please, I'll have it brought here,' Paganini replied and disappeared in the hotel lobby. A few moments later, the doorman appeared with a battered violin case and a note in the artist's own handwriting: 'Since you invited only the violin, I shall remain at home.'

*　*　*

At Clara Schumann's home on Frankfurt's Myliusstraße, an amateur violinist sawed a sonata to shreds. Pressed for his opinion Johannes Brahms, a frequent visitor in the Schumann house, stroked his beard and changed the subject. When an eager guest persisted the composer finally said: "The young man plays like our dear Clara." Perplexed at the master's lapse, the questioner hesitated: 'But Frau Schumann doesn't play the violin.' 'Neither does the young man', opined Brahms.

*　*　*

Conductor Dessoff of the Frankfurt Opera (1835-1892) disliked intensely hearing music at mealtime. At a testimonial banquet given on the occasion of his 50th birthday a string ensemble was inadvertently hired to play dinner music. After the first piece, Dessoff asked the conductor: 'Tell me, dear colleague would you mind playing something especially for me?' 'Why, it will be a pleasure, maestro, we'll play anything you like,' came the pleased reply. 'Well then, how about a game of dominoes.'

Richard Strauss was the frequent guest of a Frankfurt family who had a home on Gaertnerweg, near the opera house. He often played skat here with friends in musical circles, but one night he waited in vain for the third man who failed to keep his appointment. It was the night before Strauss was scheduled to conduct a local performance of his 'Rosenkavalier'. He asked the hostess what was playing at the opera that night and after hearing it was 'Parsifal', disappeared to make a mysterious phone call. A short time later there was knock at the door and a knight of the Holy Grail stalked across the threshold in full regalia, parked his theatrical armor and plumped down heavily at the card table. Strauss had called a singer cast in that role, knowing him to be a passable skat player, and knowing too that the knights of the Holy Grail are unemployed during the long second act.

* * *

An aging primadonna, notorious for her temperament and her failure to keep appointments had been trying the patience of opera manager Jensen. One day, the stage door attendant burst into the director's office with the message: 'The diva asks to be excused, unfortunately she cannot sing.' 'Thank heaven for small favors', the director commented wryly. 'At last she has noticed it.'

* * *

The philosopher Schopenhauer was as optimistic in his eating as he was pessimistic in his writing. One evening as he was eating his dinner at the Englischer Hof, an elegant hotel of the day, where he was a regular customer for over

27 years, another patron observed: "You eat enough for ten." To which the philosopher replied: "I think enough for ten."

* * *

Prescriptions in old Frankfurt used to carry the Latin abbreviations M. D. S. standing for *'misce, da, signa'* or 'mix, hand out and label'. A sly farmer, prescribed a potion for rheumatism, sought to pick up the doctor's trade secrets when he coupled an offer to pay his bill immediately with his question on the meaning of the mysterious letters Dr. Wegener of Frankfurt had scrawled on all his prescriptions. Amused at the farmers enterprise but also annoyed at his gumption, the noted physician announced gravely after accepting payment: "Hannes, I am not supposed to tell a patient, that M. D. S. means 'must die soon.' But you are an honest man and would not want to leave your bills unpaid."

* * *

A host of Frankfurt anecdotes are built around the person of Dr. Emil Sioli who headed the municipal insane asylum which used to be located on the grounds occupied today by the I. G. Farben Building. Siolistrasse, which runs in front of the Frankfurt American High School on those same grounds, keeps alive his memory.

The story is told that Sioli, showing a visiting colleague around the grounds of the institute, happened upon a gloomy young patient, sitting quietly under a tree, a doll cradled in his arms. 'This is our gentlest patient,' Dr. Sioli explained. 'The poor boy had a breakdown

151

when the girl he loved, went off with another fellow. He now consoles himself with the doll. In his deranged mind it has taken the place of his girl.' At that moment a raving madman burst from the bushes in a dead run, pursued by asylum attendants. He was overpowered by the wardens and lashed into a straightjacket only a few paces from Sioli. 'And this patient,' Sioli calmly turned to his visitor, 'is the fellow she ran away with.'

* * *

Although "streaking" was a recent and short-lived fad, the Frankfurt Zoo was witness to a streaker almost 100 years ago, when a middle-aged lady decided to disrobe and prance among the polar bears in her birthday suit.

* * *

Not wishing to leave the game for a single moment, a Countess Koseleff used to have her food brought to the roulette table at the Bad Homburg casino. Profiting by the wealthy countess' gambling instincts, an ingenious if crooked waiter was known to spread glue on the underside of his serving tray, managing to pick up a few gold ducats as he swished the tray elegantly over the pile of coins in front of the lady.

* * *

Eccentricity is no respector of position: Long before his death in 1772, wealthy Dr. Johann Christian Senckenberg, the city's great benefactor, had his shroud made from the bridal gown of his first wife. He also composed his own epitaph and had a habit of hop-scotching down the street instead of walking. He founded a hospital and a natural science institute, the precursor of Frankfurt university, and himself furnished the first corpse to be dissected at the institute when he fell off a scaffolding shortly before completion of the building.

When Prussian troops occupied Frankfurt in 1866, a curfew was imposed and all citizens were ordered to surrender their arms. Relations between the troops and the civilian population were anything but cordial and when a sergeant demanded of a slightly unsteady Frankfurter what he was carrying under his bulging coat, he got the pert reply 'just a sharp dagger'. 'Let's have it,' the soldier demanded. The passerby fished out a halfempty bottle of wine from his inner coat pocket, ready to have his joke on the Prussian. But the quick-witted soldier drained the bottle at a gulp and handed it back to the stunned civilian with the words: 'You may keep the scabbard.'

* * *

Also on a visit to Bad Homburg, Russian novelist Feodor Dostoyevsky jotted in his notebook in 1867: 'The situation of the spa is enchanting. The park is wonderful and so is the casino, the music is outstanding, better even than in Dresden. One could really live here if it weren't for that damned roulette.' He then hocked his watch and chain for 43 talers to pay for his trip home, promptly staked and lost the entire amount at the roulette tables. Dostoyevsky's novel 'The Gambler' was an immediate success.

* * *

On New Year's morn 1975, the Frankfurt police discovered an automobile in the Hauptwache subway station, which apparently had been driven down the steps and into the station by a reveler who had reveled a bit too much the evening before. A tow truck was dispatched to retrieve the car. During the process of pulling the car back up the steps, a passerby noticed that the stairs were being broken. Irate at the damage being done to the taxpayers' property, that good citizen reported the incident to the police. When the police again arrived on the scene, they observed that the operators of the tow truck also had reveled too much the night before, arrested them for drunken driving, and called two more tow trucks — one for the car, the other to tow away the first tow truck.

LINKS WITH THE NEW WORLD

The first noted native of Frankfurt who concerned himself with the new world was Hans Staden, author of a book published in 1557, devoted to the "Naked and Ferocious Cannibals of America". An enterprising soul, Staden spent twelve years with the Tupinambi Indians of Brazil and described their way of life in grim details. His might be called the first book on ethnology in the German language.

North America first claimed the attention of Frankfurt's important publisher's community in 1590 when Theodor de Bry brought out a German translation of Thomas Harriot's volume on Virginia, including pictures of American Indians drawn from newspaper originals de Bry had obtained in London. John White's water colors on which these etchings were based, are considered the best surviving from that period. Today they are a prize possession of the British Museum in London. The Frankfurt version of Harriot's book is dedicated to "The wild people of Virginia, discovered but recently by the British in 1585".

The first German settlers in North America were Protestants from Hesse and the Alsace who settled at Port Royal in present day South Carolina around 1562. I am sure Frankfurt would have liked to claim Peter Minuit, the shrewd tradesman who bought Manhattan from the Indians for 27 dollars—the equivalent of 60 Dutch guilders in beads, cloth and peace pipes—but he came

from Wesel on the Rhine. This prominent forbear of
New York real estate tycoons was not a Dutchman as
commonly supposed, but a Protestant deacon of his Rhineland community who escaped religious persecution by
joining the employ of the Netherlands West Indies Company. The property he bought for 27 dollars in 1626 is
now worth many billion dollars, with improvements.

King Gustav Adolf of Sweden
makes Frankfurt his Migration Headquarters

Ambitious plans for the settlement of the new world proposed by King Gustav Adolf of Sweden in the course of the
Thirty Year's War, were published in a 120-page mani-
festo by Caspar Roedtel of Frankfurt in 1633. This hand-
book for prospective settlers in North America was intended to recruit German emigrants, but even though the
project was officially supported by representatives of
four German districts who met in Frankfurt the following
year, the turmoil of war and the defeat of the Swedes
prevented the "Argonautica Gustaviana" from becoming
anything more than an ambitious project turned into
failure.

* * *

As in the case of Peter Minuit, it was again a religious
motive that was responsible for the first German settlement in America, the community of Germantown, part
of present-day Philadelphia. A few local adherents of
Protestant preacher Philip Jacob Spener, the so-called
Frankfurt Pietists, were particularly taken by the teachings of William Penn, who visited Frankfurt in August

of 1677, holding prayer-meetings in the homes of a Dutch textile merchant and the religious mystic Johanna von Merlau. Some of his Frankfurt Pietist friends apparently kept up their correspondence with Penn and, being wealthy merchants as well as converts, were soon persuaded to buy 25,000 acres of land in present-day Pennsylvania, after the British government awarded the whole region to Penn in recognition of services performed by his father, a British admiral. It was originally the intention of Frankfurt Pietists to strike out for themselves in the new world, but only one of them, attorney Franz Daniel Pastorius who practiced law in Frankfurt from 1679 to 1683, lived to see Pennsylvania. The rest rapidly lost interest as they measured the hardships of the new world against increasing comforts and diminishing persecution on the old continent. Pastorius was given a power of attorney by the Frankfurt Land Company organized by the Pietists, when he sailed on the Concord, July 24, 1683. He brought with him 33 souls collected on a recruiting trip to the Pietists' stronghold of Krefeld.

After a journey of nearly three months, the Concord reached Philadelphia on Oct 16th and Pastorius with his group quickly cleared the forest six miles from Philadelphia, built log cabins and had looms, smithies, and a mill going by next spring. The settlement, called Germantown, became the first U. S. community peopled extensively by German immigrants.

Whereas in the old country the Frankfurt Land Company came into the hand of speculators, lost its religious persuasion and was operated solely for profit, Pastorius and his friends rapidly improved their settlement. Germantown was raised to the status of township six years after its foundation, with its founder as the first mayor. Pastorius also taught school, raised bees, wrote six books and headed the first public protest against slavery in 1688. Venerated by his community, he died 68 years old in 1719. Two hundred years later a monument to his memory was unveiled in Germantown.

New York's first Governor, a Frankfurter

A fate less happy than Pastorius' was met by his contemporary, Jacob Leisler, another Frankfurt resident, whose birth certification is still preserved in the city's archives. Leisler landed in Niew Amsterdam in 1660 as a soldier in the service of the Netherlands West Indies Company. He stayed, engaged in trade and became a respected citizen of the community. During the struggle for the succession to the British throne between the Stuarts and William of Orange, Leisler and most New Yorkers sided with William against a few landowners loyal to the Stuarts. The 'Committee of Safety' which ran New York provisionally in 1689 in the absence of a legally constituted government, appointed Leisler captain "to secure the fort at New York on behalf of King William and Queen Mary". Later named Lieutenant Governor, he wielded control over New York until 1691, when a new governor with the ominous name of Sloughter was dispatched from London to take over from Leisler. Influenced against the self-made soldier-trader by his aristocratic opponents, Sloughter construed Leisler's delay in turning over the fort of New York, pending proper accreditation of the new governor as treason, had him arrested and brought before a hostile jury. Leisler was convicted of treason and hanged May 16, 1691. Noting judicial bias and the illegality of the court action, the British parliament repealed the sentence several years after Leisler's execution. Though coming too late for the governor, this vindication returned to his heirs the family's confiscated property. To Leisler, the son of a Calvinist minister of Frankfurt, belongs the credit of convoking the first congress of the American colonies when he asked the governors of Massachussetts, Plymouth, East and West Jersey, Pennsylvania, Maryland and Virginia to meet in New York in 1690 to take joint action against threatenings moves by the French colonists to the North. A Leisler statue exists in New York state. It was unveiled in 1913 by the city of New Rochelle, founded on a site he presented to Huguenot refugees, and Jakob Leisler Strasse in Frankfurt's American housing area perpetuates the memory of the local boy who became New York's first governor.

Frankfurt provides type for first German newspaper in America

A circulation list of 8,000 subscribers was reached by the first regularly-published German newspaper equipped with type cast in Frankfurt and published by Pastorius' fellow citizen of Germantown, one Chistoph Sauer. Sauer, whose descendants are active to this day in the Philadelphia publishing business, also brought out the first

German Bible printed in the States in 1743. His news-paper, called the *"Hochdeutsch Pennsylvanische Geschichts-schreiber"*, first appeared in 1739 as a calendar supplement. Though intended as a quarterly, it met so favorable a response from the German community that it was issued monthly, bi-weekly, and finally, weekly. The type foundry of Dr. Heinrich E. Luther, at that time the biggest and busiest of western Europe, supplied regular type shipments from Frankfurt to Germantown in one of the earliest of active trade relations established between the American colonies and Germany. Aided by Luther's type and using paper produced in the colonies by Wilhelm Rittinghuisen who established North America's first paper mill 1695 in Germantown, Sauer and his son turned out 160 German-language books and some 80 calendars between 1738 and 1777.

A forerunner of Sauer's first German newspaper was actually published by Ben Franklin, whose short-lived *"Piladelphische Zeitung"* saw two editions on May 6 and June 24, 1732. Franklin, who also had obtained his type from Dr. Luther visited Frankfurt in July 1768 while serving as envoy of the colonies in London, and lived in Luther's stately mansion known as "House to the Old Frog". Franklin presented Luther with an eight-inch bronze statue of himself cast in Paris showing Franklin clutching a scroll marked Pennsylvania in his right hand. Lost during World War II, the statue last appeared at the Frankfurt-America exhibit held in 1926. Franklin's 250th birthday was marked in the Frankfurt area by a front page reprint of the *"Philadelphische Zeitung"*, struck off from a historic printing press at the Gutenberg Museum of Typo-

Monument to New York's first governor, Frankfurt native son Jacob Leisler
on the New Rochelle site he presented to Huguenot refugees in 1688.

Confederate flag captured 1864 at Stilesboro, Georgia by First Lieutenant Hermann Christian Hahn, a native of Frankfurt and presented to the Frankfurt Historical Society, 1873.

Farewell of the Emigrants, 1777. Frankfurt pewter plate inscribed: Goodbye Germany, we are sailing for America. Hurrah Frankfurt.

Frankfurt-Exhibition America

MAY 2, 1926, will be the opening day of an Exhibition at Frankfort o. M. (Germany), displaying documents and mementos concerning the relationship between the Free City of Frankfort o. M. and the United States, in a commercial, historical, and financial way. The Exhibition is superintended by Professor Dr. Bernhard Müller, director of the Frankfort Historical Museum. There will be manifold evidence of the close relations, throughout centuries, between Frankfort and the United States. Earlier than any other German city, the metropolis of the Main was in touch with the new world — long before the first American Consulate was established at Frankfort, about a hundred years ago. The First National Assembly which convened at St. Paul's Church at Frankfort, was the recipient of many an address from American corporations and citizens. — Abraham Lincoln was in close connection with Frankfort bankers during his military operations. In short, the great number of points of common interest form the basis of this exhibit. A pamphlet will tell the entire history of the relationship between the United States and the former „Freie Reichsstadt", still famous for her fairs and her world-renowned commercial and scientific institutions.

IT may, justly, be assumed that this Exhibition will be of great interest to Americans, and many of them touring Germany during the coming months, will make it a point to visit it, a living proof of the friendly intercourse between the two nations during the centuries.

Poster for Frankfurt-America Exhibit, 1926.

The colors are hoisted in front of the American Consulate General in Frankfurt. The steel and glass structure erected in 1955, borders on the Palmengarten.

Philadelphische Zeitung.

SAMBSTAG, den 6 Mey. 1732.

An alle teutsche Einwohner der Provintz Pensylvanien.

NACHDEM ich von verschiedenen teutschen Einwohnern dieses Landes bin ersuchet worden, eine teutsche Zeitung ausgehen zu lassen, und ihnen darinnen das vornehmste und merckwürdigste neues, so hier und in Europa vorfallen möchte, zu communiciren; doch aber hierzu viele mühe, grosse correspondentz und auch Unkosten erfordert werden; Als habe mich entschlossen, denen teutschen zu lieb gegenwärtiges Specimen davon heraus zu geben, und ihnen dabey die Conditiones welche nothwendig zu der continuation derselben erfordert werden, bekent zu machen.

Erstlich, müsten zum wenigsten, um die unkosten die darauf lauffen, gut zu machen, 300 stücks können gedruckt und debitiret werden, und müste in jeder Township dazu ein mann ausgemachet werden, welcher mir wissen liesse, wie viel Zeitungen jedes mahl an ihn müsten gesandt werden, und der sie dan weiter seinen jeglichen zustellen und die bezahlung davor einfordern müste.

Vor jede Zeitung muss jährlich 10 Shillinge erleget, und davon alle quartal 2 sh. 6 d. bezahlet werden.

Dagegen verspreche ich auf meiner seite, durch gute Correspondentz die ich in Holland und England habe alle zeit das merkwürdigste und neueste so in Europa und auch hier passiret, alle wocne einmahl, nemlich Sonnabends in gegenwärtiger form einer Zeitung, nebst denen schiffen so hier abgehen und ankommen, und auch das steigen oder fallen des Preisses der Guter, und was sonst zu wissen dienlich bekandt zu machen.

Advertissemente oder Bekant machungen, welche man an mich schicken möchte, sollen das erste mahl vor 3 shill. 3 mahl aber vor 5 shil: hinein gesetzet werden.

Und weil ich nützlich erachte die gantze beschreibung der aufrichtung dieser provintz, mit allen derselben privilegien, rechten und gesetzen, bey ermangelung genugsamer Neuigkeiten, darinnen bekandt zu machen; solte nicht undienlich seyn, dass ein jeder, zumahl wer kinder hat, diese Zeitungen wohl bewahre, und am ende des jahres an einander heffte; zumahl da solche dann gleichsam als eine Chronica dienen können, die vorigen Geschichte daraus zu ersehen, und die folgende desto besser zu verstehen.

Auch wird anbey zu bedencken gegeben, ob es nicht rahtsam wäre, in jeder grossen Township einen reitenden Boten zu bestellen, welcher alle woche einmahl nach der stadt reiten und was in jeder da zu bestellen hat, mit nehmen könne.

So bald nun die obgemeldte anzahl der Unterschreiber vorhanden, welche so bald als möglich ersuche in Philadelphia

America's first German-language newspaper published by Benjamin Franklin, using type obtained from Dr. Ehrenfried Luther's foundry in Frankfurt.

graphy in Mainz and distributed to German bibliophiles throughout the world.

The Methodist Church of America, first organized in Ohio in 1785, owes much to Peter Boehler, son of a Frankfurt brewer who met church founder John Wesley in London, while en route to the colonies as a missionary of the Moravian Brethren in 1783. Wesley was converted by Boehler and visited Germany the following year to study the teaching of the Moravian Protestant group, headed by Count Zinzendorf who had dispatched Boehler on his missionary activities. During his stay in Frankfurt Wesley lived with Boehler's father. Boehler the missionary, who had a decisive influence on the founder of Methodism, did not linger in London long but continued on to Georgia according to his instructions. Little is known here of his life in the States.

Jefferson in Frankfurt

Dwight Eisenhower was not the only American President who spent some time in Frankfurt before becoming chief executive. Thomas Jefferson visited Frankfurt in 1788 during his tenure as Minister to France, reporting that "I am continually amused by seeing here the origin of whatever is not English among us. I have fancied myself often in the upper parts of Maryland and Pennsylvania". In his diary Jefferson states that he visited two of his former German prisoners during the revolutionary war, Barons von Geismar and von Unger, while staying in Frankfurt and vicinity between April 6 and 14, 1788. Jefferson, who traveled the continent to look and to listen, made copious notes on agriculture and industrial improvements for possible application in the young republic, and took a great interest in the culture and preparation of the famed Hochheim wine. He purchased a hundred vine shoots carrying them back to Paris for planting in his garden. They took easily to the new soil, sprouting new branches, and Jefferson voiced hopes of taking them back to America. "If you ever revisit Monticello", he wrote von Geismar with keen satisfaction, "I shall be able to give you there a glass of Hock or Ruedesheim of my own making".

He was less complimentary of Germany's political and religious institutions. Though he looked at the Palatinate as being "a second mother country" to America, for it was from here that "those swarms of Germans have gone, who next to the descendants of the English form the greatest body of our people", he decried the visible signs of religious and political persecution in Germany. On entering Prussia from Holland, he wrote in his diary, he was struck by the sudden transition from ease and opulence to extreme poverty. Soil and climate were the same, the answer, he noted, must be a difference in government, the former liberal, the latter an absolute monarchy. He detected "slavish fear in the faces of the Prussians", the oppression of Protestants by the prevailing Catholic government of Cologne and oppression of Catholics by the Protestant government of Frankfurt. German newspapers of the period seem to have sensed the uncomplimentary attitude of the American visitor or considered his presence too unimportant, at any rate he is not mentioned with a single line in the 'arrival and departures' column of the Frankfurt newspaper preserved from that period.

On a dark and cloudy afternoon in November 1963, thousands of Frankfurt citizens gathered in the pouring rain at the Roemer. They were drawn by the magnetic memory of President John F. Kennedy, who at that moment was being taken to his burial place in Arlington National Cemetary. Barely 5 month earlier, on the 25th of June, he captured the hearts of Frankfurt's citizens during his historic visit to the coronation city of the German emperors.

After signing his name in the Golden Book in the historic Kaisersaal at the Roemer, Kennedy spoke to the many thousand gathered on the Roemerberg. In his well-remembered, informal way he related how, en route to Frankfurt his traveling companions, the Federal Chancellor and the Hessian Minister President were pointing out individuals along the way as being respectively CDU or SPD party members. But Kennedy commented that he could not determine any real difference; he had the feeling they were all friends. After the enthusiastic response of the crowd, Kennedy departed from his scheduled walk to the Paulskirche and for a few moments broke away from the Secret Service and security police in order to mix and shake hands with the people.

Later in the Paulskirche Kennedy made a major policy speech, which was called by the Frankfurt press a "policy statement of the President in his capacity as the leader of the Western World" and a "dialogue with all the peoples and powers of the world".

A plaque at the Paulskirche commemorates Kennedy's visit to Frankfurt. Forsthausstrasse, the main thoroughfare from Frankfurt to Frankfurt Flughafen, over which Kennedy departed Frankfurt, is now known as Kennedy Allee in his honor.

Frankfurt Consulates in the USA

The Free City of Frankfurt maintained its own consular representatives in the United States until annexed by Prussia in 1866. At one time Frankfurt consulates were operating in New York, Philadelphia, Cincinnati, Chicago, St. Louis and Milwaukee. The earliest of these was established 1826 in Philadelphia, the last one in Milwaukee during 1858. The Frankfurt consuls issued passports, reported on trade and, under prevailing agreements with the other sovereign German states, handled consular matters of the nationals of all German states except for those maintaining their own mission in the area. Frankfurt consulates fostered a favorable climate for trade relations between the two countries by enthusiastic reports on business opportunities, government stability and expansion prospects of the growing American economy. Themselves recruited largely from the ranks of German immigrants, the consular representatives unanimously voiced their support of Lincoln and the North in the sectional differences preceding the outbreak of the Civil War. When hostilities started, they forecast a Union victory from the beginning. Coupled with the efforts of U. S. Consul General William Walton

Murphy in Frankfurt, their reports on the solvency of the Union contributed materially to the placement of Union securities and obligations on the Frankfurt Stock Exchange, at that time the biggest trading center on the continent for the issues of the North.

The U. S. Consulate General in Frankfurt

In 1829, three years after Frankfurt's first Consulate in the U. S. was established at Philadelphia, President John Quincy Adams appointed Ernst Schwendler, a German-American resident of the Free City as U. S. Consul in Frankfurt. Schwendler had lived for years in Philadelphia after going to the States in the employ of a silk export house in 1805 and was probably proposed for the consular post by Frankfurt's representative in Pennsylvania, a state to which he was linked by numerous business affiliations. He served till his death in 1853 at the age of 77, but was forced into semi-retirement by ill health during the last ten years of his life. His early years as Consul were mainly devoted to the fostering of commercial relations with the USA and the counselling of emigrants who left Frankfurt in considerable numbers after the ill-fated revolt of 1833.

By the time 1848 rolled around, Major Andrew Jackson Donelson, diplomatic representative of the U. S. at the provisional central authority, which governed Germany from Frankfurt for one year, wrote in his despatches "the local American Consul, who is very old and by gout chained to his armchair, is as anxious as unable to do his duty". Under Louisiana's Samuel Ricker, appointed Consul in 1853 following the death of Schwendler, the Frankfurt post became a Consulate General, and was enlarged to include the Free Cities of Hamburg, Bremen and Luebeck. Sam Ricker's official activities found a sudden end at the outbreak of the Civil War when the outspoken Southerner was replaced by President Lincoln with William Walton Murphy. But Ricker remained in Frankfurt as a private citizen and caused no end of trouble for Murphy by his activities in behalf of the Confederacy. Ricker even succeeded in placing a loan for the Confederate States, but Murphy won out in obtaining almost unanimous support of Frankfurt bankers and the officials of the Free City. Even so, evidence in the National Archives suggests that Mr. Ricker and Mr. Murphy kept in fairly close touch with each other. For example, Mr. Ricker wrote one of Mr. Murphy's first economic reports. Mr. Murphy spent a lot of time helping Mr. Ricker obtain reimbursement for materials he had supplied the Consulate General. And the microfilms of the Consulate General's files even show a letter from Mr. Murphy's Vice Consul, Mr. Charles Graebe, attesting to the fact that Mr. Ricker was not and had not been a secessionist.

To give public proof that he represented the whole Union, not only the northern states, Murphy requested and received permission to hoist Old Glory over his official residence at Weserstrasse 19. Largely through Murphy's efforts, Frankfurt traders staked their faith and finances in the Union, buying up some $ 600 million of U. S. war bonds and debentures. Murphy was extremely active during the eight years of his Frankfurt assignment. Besides penning pamphlets and articles in support of the fund-raising activities of the Union at the Frankfurt Stock Exchange, he exchanged frequent letters with the city council on export and trade regulations and sent detailed weekly reports to Washington on the Frankfurt money and credit market.

Frankfurt archives note that this penchant for raising flags in honor of visiting dignitaries made him the center of a diplomatic incident in 1863, when he ran up the Mexican flag next to the Stars and Stripes to greet the Emperor of Austria whose brother Maximilian then ruled that country. Francis Joseph of Austria had convoked a meeting of German kings, dukes and princes as a final attempt to unite the German states and solve the differences between Austria and Prussia. The French emissary to the National Assembly in Frankfurt termed Murphy's flag-raising gesture an unfriendly act, because France was at war with Mexico. He complained bitterly about his American colleague and Murphy had no choice but to haul down the Mexican flag in a hurry and write a long letter of explanation to the Frankfurt City Council in which he deplored the excessive sensitivity of the French minister plenipotentiary. Since Murphy's days there have been 29 consuls general in Frankfurt, and the offices of the consulate have moved a dozen times until a modern functional building was erected in 1955 according to plans of the New York architectural firm of Skidmore Owings and Merrill, creators of the Lever Brothers building on Park Avenue, of which the Frankfurt consulate is a miniature. The five-story glass-enclosed structure includes on its grounds the "Hextopus", a stabile by the noted American

U.S. Consuls General at Frankfurt

Ernst Schwendler (1829—1853)
Samuel Ricker (1854-1861)
William Walton Murphy (1861-1869)
William Prentis Webster (1869-1877)
Alfred E. Lee (1877-1881)
Ferdinand K. W. Vogeler (1881-1885)
Jacob Mueller (1885-1889)
Frank H. Mason (1889-1899)
Richard Guenther (1899-1910)
Frank D. Hill (1910-1912)
Heaton W. Harris (1912-1917)
John R. Wood (1920-1922)
Fred E. T. Dumont (1922-1925)
Christian Ravndal (1925-1926)
Hamilton Claiborne (1926-1928)
Robert W. Heingartner (1928)
Edward A. Dow (1928-1930)
Felix Cole (1930-1931)
Will L. Lowry (1931-1933)
George A. Mackinson (1934-1936)
Emil Sauer (1936-1940)
Sydney B. Redecker (1940-1941) (1946-1948)
Marshall M. Vance (1948-1950)
Albert Doyle (1950-1952)
C. Montagu Pigott (1952-1955)
John H. Burns (1955-1957)
W. Wendell Blancke (1957-1960)
Edmund J. Dorsz (1961-1963)
Henry H. Ford (1963-1965)
James R. Johnstone (1965-1970)
Robert H. Harlan (1971-1975)
Wolfgang J. Lehmann (since 1975)

sculptor Alexander Calder. A good many of the American consuls who served in Frankfurt during the 150-year history of this oldest U. S. consulate general in Germany were later appointed ambassadors of their country and reached high diplomatic honors. A list of the American consuls serving in Frankfurt since Ernst Schwendler first put up his shingle in 1829, is appended to this chapter.

Location of American Consulates in Frankfurt

1829-1853	Haus Schoene Aussicht 17	1899-1928	Schillerstrasse 20
1861-1869	Weserstrasse 19	1928-1931	Boersenstrasse 2-4
1869-1877	Goetheplatz	1931-1941	Kaiserstrasse 27
1877-1881	Mainzer Landstrasse 21	1945-1952	Bockenheimer Anlage 11
1881-1885	Kaiserstrasse 10	1952-1955	Bockenheimer Anlage 13
1885-1889	Kaiserstrasse 26	1955-present	Siesmayerstrasse 21
1889-1899	Mainzer Landstrasse 21		

Frankfurt Boys make good as U. S. Generals and Diplomats

The assertion that Frankfurt is a good place to be *from*, which crops up with unkindly frequency in discussions about the weather, has found proof positive in the careers of Frankfurt citizens. Short-term residents and the native-born whose spirit of adventure made them seek their fortune in America, regularly went on to bigger things from here. Gustav Peter Koerner, Lt. Governor of Illinois, 1852-1856; U.S. Ambassador to Spain, 1862-1864; co-founder of the Republican Party, left his native city of Frankfurt as a 24-year-old-student, disguised in woman's clothes to get past the roadblocks thrown up around the city in search of participants in the abortive student revolt. After his successful flight to the States, he practiced law in Illinois and became a close friend of President Lincoln, who frequently sought his advice on German questions. Before taking on the delicate mission of keeping Spain neutral in the Civil War, he helped to organize the 24th Infantry Regiment of Illinois and served in the Union army as a colonel. The city he fled as an outlaw 30 years before gave Koerner an overwhelming reception when he stopped here on his way to Spain in 1862. He wrote his children 'Frankfurt now looks like America, with freedom of movement, active trade and a lively atmosphere'. Koerner's ties to Germany remained strong even after he returned to the States. A book of Spanish experiences was published in Frankfurt and his life's work was crowned with the publication of a volume on "The German Element in the United States of America from 1818-1848". Koerner who lived to the ripe old age of 87, described himself in his memoirs as 'a son of the free city of Frankfurt in which each cobblestone has its history'.

Another U. S. ambassador born near Frankfurt where he spent the formative years of his life was August Belmont, clerk in the Frankfurt banking house of Rothschild & Co. Born 1806 in Alzey, Rheinhessen, Belmont quickly developed a penchant for travel, banking and politics, leaving for the U. S. from Naples where he lived after 1833 as branch office chief of the Rothschild firm. He was perhaps the only man to be given top diplomatic assignments by two countries with vastly differing political systems within the short space of three years. Until 1849 Belmont served as consul general of Austria in New York. In 1852 he was appointed U.S. ambassador to the Netherlands, a position he held for five years. Belmont participated actively in the political life of his adopted country in a career climaxed by his chairmanship of the Democratic National Committee from 1860-1872.

Like the ambassadors, U.S. generals of German origin distinguished themselves in American history. During the Civil War, Brigadier General George W. Mindel of N.Y., one of 500 first-generation German immigrants who fought on the side of the Union, personally led a Union charge that silenced the Confederate artillery in the battle of Williamsburgh. Mindel commanded New York's famed 27th Infantry Regiment as a colonel, was later promoted to brigadier general on the staffs of McClellan and Kearney, and was put in charge of a brigade of five regiments, while marching through Georgia with General Sherman.

Adolf Engelmann, another Frankfurter, headed the German volunteer regiment of Illinois, was appointed brigadier general and won numerous citations for personal bravery. He was a brother of botanist George Engelmann who wrote on the cactii of North America, studying the fauna of the Far West on long horseback trips through prairies and mountain ranges away from his home in St. Louis. George practiced medicine, later specialized in botany and was appointed president of the Academy of Science. Noted also as a publisher, he brought out the two-volume work on the flora in Texas compiled by a fellow Frankfurter, Ferdinand Jacob Lindheimer. Engelmann also published a German periodical called *West-land,* dedicated to supplying new and prospective immigrants with factual accounts of western living and working conditions instead of the fictional and dramatized renderings in vogue at that period.

Frankfurt's historical museum still owns a Confederate flag captured by native son Hermann Christian Hahn while serving as a Union soldier in 1864. Hahn sent the flag to his father in the old country, who passed it on in 1876 to the Frankfurt historical society.

Wisconsin's Governor passes declining years on Grueneburgweg

Edward Salomon, organizer of the 26th Wisconsin Infantry Regiment and later governor of the state until 1868, was one of four German immigrant brothers, two of whom later became generals in the U.S. Army. Salomon, a prominent lawyer, distinguished himself in the Indian wars, and was later elected chief executive of Wisconsin. After he stepped down from the governorship, Salomon practiced law in New York and moved to Frankfurt in 1894. He lived at Gruneburgweg 125, until his death in 1909.

Frankfurt's Stock Exchange Plays Role in U.S. History

New York and Frankfurt stock exchanges have a curious parallel in their development; both started under the open sky and moved through a succession of temporary quarters on the road to becoming the main financial centers of their respective nations. The trading posts of the present Frankfurt Exchange, opened in February 1957, are linked with the main financial centers of the world by 700 telephone and 100 teletype lines. The course of the 168 officially traded stocks is displayed on an electronic board approximately 1,000 square feet in area. It had humbler beginnings.

In 1585, Frankfurt merchants first met on Roemerberg square to negotiate credit transactions. Nearly two hundred years later, in 1792 their New York colleagues first met under an old buttonwood tree on Wall Street. The securities business in Frankfurt dates from the time the Bethmann Bros., court bankers of Empress Maria Theresia, first started trading in government obligations. Before that time the open-air meetings of Frankfurt traders served mainly the purpose of credit and foreign exchange transactions. After the Frankfurt Exchange finally moved into a permanent building in 1843, active trading started in overseas bond and stock issues known as the 'exotics'. This expansion took place partly as a result of the international connections of the Rothschild banking family, natives of Frankfurt since the 17th century. The Exchange building was the sensation of the day with its Moorish columns, intricate ceiling decorations and North African exterior. The Rothschild brothers, who helped found Frankfurt's international banking reputation, were in their seventies when the Stock Exchange opened. Owning important private banks in London, Paris, Vienna, Naples, and Frankfurt, much of the continent's credit transactions became a family affair, and

America began to enter the picture after the aforementioned August Belmont, later U. S. Ambassador to the Netherlands, opened a Rothschild branch office in New York in 1837.

When Frankfurt's colorful Amschel Meyer Rothschild died in 1855 at the age of 82, he is reputed to have told his nephews on his deathbed: "the Lord is getting me at 18 below par". With his immense wealth, he figures as a central character in numerous anecdotes and is once said to have told the questioner who asked why his speculations always turned out so successful, "I use my speculations like an ice-cold bath; quickly in, quickly out".

During the Civil War it was Consul General William W. Murphy who succeeded in influencing Frankfurt traders to stake their faith in finances in the Union to the tune of $ 600 million in U. S. government obligations. A number of New York firms established by German immigrants trekked back to the old country with branch offices and participated actively in placing U. S. government securities on the Frankfurt Exchange. Among them were the New York firms of Seligmann & Stettheimer, Lazard, Speyer-Ellissen and Hallgarten & Co., backers of U. S. civil war debentures and to this day members of the New York Stock Exchange. At one time between 1861 and 1864, six different U. S. government issues were actively traded on the Frankfurt Exchange, and a New York Times correspondent wrote in August 1864 that "several hundred Frankfurt brokers shouted themselves hoarse for the American securities".

In a time of grave financial crisis, when six per cent U. S. government bonds fell to a value of 45 dollars on the hundred, and the federal debt increased from 1.7 to 2.7 billion dollars within a year, the Frankfurt Exchange helped the Union finance the war. It was responsible in no small part for re-establishing the trust of the major European powers in the solvency of the Union, after the issues of the Confederacy were initially favored by the major exchanges in Britain and on the Continent.

"From the first to last Frankfurt on the Main stood firmly by us", U.S. Ambassador to Germany Andrew D. White stated at memorial observances in Berlin around the turn of the century, describing the Frankfurt exchange as "the most beneficial center of financial influences". The trust Frankfurt bankers placed in the cause of the Union was repaid in full when all war obligations were honored at par after the war. Some of the money deriving from these transactions was again invested by Frankfurt brokers in American railway issues which played a substantial part in opening the Far West. Bethmann Bros. placed the 1887 issues of the Chicago, Burlington and Quincy railroad and the 1889 stocks of the San Francisco and North Pacific railway. Groups of underwriters in Frankfurt also took part in the financing of the first transatlantic cable, and in the placing of many Latin American issues. Each year, several hundred million dollars worth of overseas securities found buyers here until Frankfurt gradually lost out to Berlin as Germany's major exchange, during the last years of the 19th century.

Voicing his personal gratitude to Frankfurt banker families for their support of the Union cause, President Lincoln sent christening spoons and gifts of books to a

Frankfort a. Maine
March 24th 1870.

Mr Phillipp. N. Schmidt
    My dear Sir:
                    Feeling
assured that you were a great
friend & admirer of my
beloved husband, may I
request your acceptance
of this bust, which I con-
-sider a very true likeness
I remain, most respectfully
            Mrs Lincoln.

Letter of Mary Todd Lincoln presenting a marble bas-relief of her husband to Frankfurt banker Philipp Nikolaus Schmidt.

number of prominent Frankfurt financiers just prior to his tragic death from the bullets of a demented assassin. In 1870, his widow Mary Todd Lincoln visited Frankfurt, leaving a relief cast of her husband's countenance as a present with a family friend, the noted local banker Philipp Nikolaus Schmidt. This marble bas-relief and her letter to Schmidt are still in the possession of Frankfurt's Historical Museum to which they were given in 1926 by the banker's descendants.

The hero of the Union armies, General Ulysses S. Grant, president of the United States for two successive terms, likewise paid a visit to Frankfurt to voice his personal gratitude to Leopold Sonnemann, publisher of the *Frankfurter Zeitung,* the largest and most influential daily of the German-speaking area that had steadfastly pleaded the Union cause. It had reported extensively on the military campaigns of the Union, published lead editorials in support of President Lincoln's emancipation policies and called on German financial circles to back U.S. bond issues. With the same editorial intent, the *Frankfurter Zeitung* fought efforts of Confederate agents — among them Sam Ricker — to find markets in Germany for the 'Cotton Loan', floated by the Confederacy.

During his tour of Europe after retiring from the Presidency, U.S. Grant arrived in Frankfurt July 15, 1877 'to shake Sonnemann's hand' and to visit the city that had done so much for the Union cause. According to Sonnemann's memoirs, the president and the publisher had a long private talk and strolled together in the Palmengarten the day of his arrival. Grant stayed in Frankfurt for three days, and was tendered an official reception by the city. Lord Mayor von Mumm welcomed the U. S. President and army hero at the city hall and the retired Consul General Murphy recalled the sympathies which had always prevailed in Frankfurt for the cause of the Republic, especially for anti-slavery moves by official and private groups throughout the United States. The women of Frankfurt, he said, were the first ones to take up a collection for the wounded of the Civil War.

In the official reply to the Mayor's welcoming address, General Grant thanked the citizens of the ancient Free City of Frankfurt for the confidence they had placed in the United States during those critical days when they had freely staked their property in the cause of the Republic.

After the Free City of Frankfurt was annexed by Prussia in 1866, the Frankfurt Stock Exchange gradually lost its place to Berlin as the primary financial center of Germany, though trading remained lively until the start of World War II. The last president of the exchange, until the Nazi take-over in 1933 was Oskar Oppenheimer, owner of a banking firm of the same name which was founded in the last century as the branch office of a New York banking concern. Badly damaged during the war, the Frankfurt Exchange has now regained its traditional place as Germany's leading stock market.

Texas narrowly skirts fate
of becoming Frankfurt dependency

This may come as a shock to genuine Texans but it seems that the history of a good part of the hill country, at least in its early stages, was made in Frankfurt by Frankfurters. While Texas was a republic following Sam Houston's successful revolt against Mexico in 1836, a group of German noblemen, centered in the Frankfurt area, dispatched German colonists in large numbers to the hill country near San Antonio as Step One of their plan to make the young republic a dependent state under the protectorate of German princes. Known as the Mainz Nobles' Association, - *Mainzer Adelsverein* - its membership roster read like the German version of 'Burke's Peerage', or the cast of a Sigmund Romberg operetta. It included the reigning dukes of Nassau, Meiningen, Coburg-Gotha, Prince Frederick of Prussia, the princes of Wied, Solms-Braunfels, Leiningen, Schwarzburg-Rudolstadt, and the counts of Isenburg-Meerholz, and Alt- und Neu-Leiningen.

Playing unintentionally into the hands of the nobles, a Mr. Daingerfield, at that time Minister of the Republic of Texas at The Hague, undertook to encourage German emigration by sponsoring a land-settlement agent in Frankfurt. But the Free City looked askance at the activities of the nobles and their efforts to lure its good citizens into the uncertainties of the new world, away from the relative comforts and security of the prospering trading center. A ruling by the city council prohibited Mr. Daingerfield from opening a recruiting office for Texas colonists in the city of Frankfurt. Many meetings of the Mainz Nobles' Association took place nonetheless in the city, and prominent Frankfurt bankers financially underwrote the organization with more than one million guilders—the equivalent of half a million dollars. Headed by a charter member of the nobles' group, Prince Karl zu Solms-Braunfels, about two hundred immigrants founded the town of New Braunfels on Good Friday, 1845. The prince was appointed Commissioner General of the 'Society for the Protection of German Immigrants in Texas' as the *Adelsverein* called itself in the new world, and he purchased the site of the town on behalf of the association for 1.111 dollars from the Garza family of San Antonio. The oddities of New Braunfels became legendary in the hill-country. Prince Karl surrounded himself with a retinue of velvet-clad courtiers and officers sporting cocked hats, received Indians in the full-dress uniform of the Austrian Army, and publicly proclaimed his intention of remaining outside the U. S., which was then moving to incorporate the Republic as the 28th state of the Union. Ratified by popular vote, the incorporation took place October 13, 1845. Meanwhile, more immigrants whose trip to America was financed by the *Adelsverein* were landed at Indianola, then the most active and important of Texas seaports. Busy Karl had founded Indianola some years earlier, naming it Karlshafen, in honor of himself. Through Indianola passed most of the commerce and immigration of Texas until 1875, when the thriving port of 7,000 was wrecked in a gulf storm. In the years that followed, the survivors moved away and the gulf port passed out of existence. All that remains of Indianola today are a few concrete foundations and a decaying cemetery. Prince Karl resigned his post as Commissioner General in 1845 and returned to Germany following the annexation of Texas. Before his hurried departure, he lived in grand style at his hilltop fortress called Sophienburg after his wife. Over his castle flew the flags of Austria in deference to the uniform he wore, and that of the Republic of Texas. Solms-Braunfels' followers suffered privations and hardships in the unaccustomed environment. Supplies failed to reach the settlement in the confusion of the Mexican War, epidemics took their toll of the colonists, and the Nobles Association foundered in 1853, when their properties were assigned to Texas creditors. The surviving settlers finally weathered the battle with disease and the elements and succeeded in establishing several flourishing communities, including Frederiksburg, Boerne and Berheim. Today, the German influence in New Braunfels remains unmistakable. German is still taught along with English in the public schools, and German signs are common on shops and signboards. To this day, lively relations are being maintained with Braunfels near Frankfurt. Several hundred New Braunfels townsfolk came over in 1957 in a mass visit to the city of their forefathers. A Frankfurt botanist, Ferdinand Jakob Lindheimer helped in the hard pioneer days to put New Braunfels on its feet again. He fought with Sam Houston at San Jacinto, after coming to Texas in the wake of the ill-fated Frankfurt student revolt that brought a group of talented young men to the shores of the new world. Surveying Texas on horseback like Engelmann in the far west, he charted the fauna and flora of the new state discovering many previously unknown plants of which some were named after him. In 1850, Lindheimer was made New Braunfels' Justice of the Peace and two years later founded there Texas' first German newspaper. He edited and published the *Neu*

Braunfels Zeitung until his death in 1879, at the age of 70. Not all Frankfurters who came to New Braunfels had as creditable a record as Dr. Lindheimer. Another doctor, Theodor Koester, Frankfurt general practitioner, who had flunked his medical exams before barely skimming by on the second try, emigrated to New Braunfels in 1842. He practiced his profession in a fashion that caused the New Braunfels cemetery to be popularly known as "Koester's plantation".

Dinosaur Spans the Atlantic

Family contacts established between Frankfurt and America in later years also benefited the educational and scientific institutes of the city. New York scions of Frankfurt banking families, like Jakob H. Schiff and James

Skeleton of 72 ft
dinosaur 'diplodocus longus'
on view at the Senckenberg Museum.
Gift of the American Museum
of Natural History, New York, 1907.

Speyer, donated large sums to Frankfurt University, and the former dispatched the skeleton of the giant mastodon, 'Americanus Kerr', as a gift to the Senckenberg foundation at the opening of its new museum building in 1907. At that time the President of the American Museum of Natural History in N. Y., Morris K. Jessup, gave the Senckenberg Museum an intact skeleton of the rare dinosaur 'Diplodocus Longus'. The 72 foot antediluvian, startling visitors in the entrance hall of the Frankfurt museum is the only one of its kind on view in Europe. The Senckenberg Natural History Museum also obtained many gifts of American explorers of German origin who helped chart the plant and animal life of the new world, among them Dr. Engelmann, whose exploits have already been listed. Senckenberg is specially noted for its collection of American fossils.

* * *

The America department of the city library was another testimonial to the close relations between Frankfurt and the U. S. before World War One. In 1905, the constituting meeting of the "Committee for the Establishment of an American Section in the Municipal Library of Frankfurt on the Main, Germany" took place. The committee, composed of prominent German-Americans, among them banker Charles L. Hallgarten, donated 40,000 marks for the purchase of American books and corresponded with government offices, universities, and scientific societies in the United States in successful efforts to obtain literary, legal and scientific volumes. By 1908, the America section of the city library already owned 4,500 books, and by 1926, the America section had doubled its inventory to about 9,000 volumes. But except for some legal books which survived destruction, the America section of the city library became a victim of World War II. Its place has been taken by the many thousands of books by American authors dealing with American life, on the open shelves of the Frankfurt *Amerika Haus.*

New Links since the War

From its modest beginning in November 1945 as an American Reading Room established for the German population, the Frankfurt Amerika Haus has become an established institution and an integral part of the city's intellectual life. Operated by the U. S. Information Agency in a modern city-built structure at the edge of the municipal Rothschild Park in downtown Frankfurt, the center has become a bridge which has been crossed over the years by many thousands of visitors from both lands.

As is true in all Amerika Houses in Germany, it serves its function as a place of open discourse and as a resource for those who wish to explore American thought through the library, and the many facets of American culture through exhibits and presentations. The spirit of furthering friendship and understanding between the two peoples and of stimulating and promoting a German-American dialogue on problems of mutual concern has remained unchanged throughout the thirty years of its existence.

In 1975, with an emphasis on modern communications techniques, the Amerika Haus was thoroughly modernized in appearance, in programming capabilities and services offered. The auditorium, the most advanced "studio" in Frankfurt, can be used for multi-media programs, workshops, seminars and concerts, as well as for film and theater performances. The library, making use of the newest ideas in library science, offers the most up-to-date information possible. A collection of some 500 American periodicals, received regularly by airmail, help insure this result.

The American way of life is also on view daily at the many U. S. military housing projects in and around Frankfurt, built to accomodate the innumerable short-term military residents who have passed through here since the war. Undoubtedly the most famous of these was President Dwight D. Eisenhower. His offices were located on the first floor of the I. G. Farben Building, from 1945-46, while he served here as Allied Expeditionary Force Supreme Commander and Commanding General of the U. S. Forces, European Theater. A conference room in the building is named in his honor.

During the Potsdam conference in July 1945, the 26th to be exact, President Harry S. Truman visited General Eisenhower in his Frankfurt headquarters. Arriving at Rhein Main airport, the president of the U. S. toured the city in an open car, inspecting units of the Third Armored Division whose men had been posted all along the thirty mile route. The day-long visit also took President Truman to Heppenheim and Weinheim, the latter headquarters of the 84th Infantry Division commanded by Major General A. G. Bolling. The historic scene of Harry Truman inspecting the honor guard to the tune of the 'Missouri Waltz', recorded for posterity on newsreels shown around the world, was enacted at Heppenheim near Darmstadt. In his memoirs, President Truman notes that he ended his

America Haus, erected by the city of Frankfurt in 1957 and operated by the U. S. Information Agency.

brief talk to the troops "by telling them that I did not want to keep them in the hot sun to listen to me any longer since I was not running for office and since they couldn't vote for me anyway".

In the afternoon of July 26th, the President returned to the headquarters building in Frankfurt, on whose preservation amidst the general destruction he comments in his memoirs. His talk with General Eisenhower in the Frankfurt headquarters building, previously occupied by the main offices of the I. G. Farben chemicals trust, was the first and probably only time two successive U. S. Presidents met on German soil.

In later years, the constructive approach to German problems and the tactfulness displayed by John J. McCloy, the first civilian High Commissioner who also made his headquarters in Frankfurt after the war, helped West German authorities regain their self-respect in the transition from occupation to self-government. To the middle class McCloy home in suburban Bad Homburg flocked professors, political leaders, artists and trade unionists for the informal lunches several times a week that provided the basis for a real exchange of opinions and helped McCloy to become the most popular of top-level Americans in occupied Germany.

For most of his three-year tenure in Germany from 1949 to 1952, High Commissioner McCloy maintained his offices at the I. G. Farben building in Frankfurt in the belief that in all likelihood Frankfurt would became the capital of the emerging West German government. The High Commission moved away from Frankfurt early in 1952 after Bonn was selected as capital, and the new Embassy building was built there on the banks of the Rhine.

During his tenure in Germany, McCloy helped make available and supervised the injection of more than a billion dollars worth of U. S. aid into the German economy. Coupled with hard work, perseverance and self-denial on a national scale, American economic aid sparked the industrial boom that transformed the German economy from rags to riches in an unprecedented few years.

But McCloy is best remembered in Frankfurt for the millions of marks in U. S. taxpayers' money that went by his initiative into rebuilding universities, setting up truly independent newspapers, helping students' and old peoples homes, and priming the reconstruction of priceless cultural shrines like the *Goethe Haus*.

The postwar contacts with American thoughts, motivations and techniques which McCloy helped pioneer are still increasing in a world that grows smaller daily. With Frankfurt serving as the major German air terminal, most U. S. business firms operating in Geramny have clustered around the Frankfurt region. The city's position in the geographical center of West Germany, the international trade fairs, and the concentration of banking and finance may also be responsible; at any rate hundreds of the largest U. S. firms maintain branch offices in and around the city. They include movie distributors, banks, airlines, advertising agencies, and car manufacturers, who have joined forces as Frankfurt's American Chamber of Commerce in Germany. In 1962 the United States Government, recognizing the importance of the growing market in Germany, opened the U. S. Trade Center in Frankfurt. Since the first exhibition in November 1962, which featured electrical applicances, the U. S. Trade Center has been the site for over 100 U. S. Government sponsored shows. American manufacturers of such diverse products as geophysical equipment, nuclear instrumentation, minicomputers, and pumps, valves, and compressors have been able to generate sales totalling hundreds of million of dollars, and have firmly established themselves in the German market by acquiring representation here, through their participation in the export promotion activities of the U. S. Trade Center. The Center has also been used by scores of German representatives of U. S. companies to exhibit goods between regularly scheduled exhibitions; for conferences, seminars, and sales meetings. The Trade Center continues to play an important role in the U. S.' program to expand exports in its third largest market; the Federal Republic's imports from the U. S. were estimated at $ 5.5 billion in 1974. The Trade Center is centrally located in Frankfurt just across from the old Opera House.

German-American relation on an informal basis are fostered by the Steuben Schurz Society, a socially-active group, several hundred strong that sponsors dances, exhibits and excursions to acquaint the short-term American residents of the city with old-line Frankfurt families. The motto is international understanding, and the name of the society attests its orientation towards the best in German-American relations: General Friedrich Wilhelm von Steuben who trained Washington's armies contributed decisively to the victories of the young republic; Carl Schurz, German student leader in 1848 revolt, later U. S. Senator from Missouri became the outstanding German-American of the 19th century.

Frankforts in America

A study of the postal service ZIP code directory and the latest Rand McNally road atlas yielded 18 separate Frankforts and Frankfords in the USA, ranging in size from 21,000 downwards. They are spread from Maine to Kansas, and from Alabama to South Dakota. Ontario also boasts a Frankford, with nearly 2,000 proud citizens. Illinois takes the prize for the most Frankforts, having three — Frankfort, West Frankfort and Frankfort Heights.

The most venerable among them no doub is the suburb of Philadelphia, founded in 1685, two years after Germantown, most of the rest were settled in the 18th and

19th centuries. The state capital of Kentucky is among them, and is the largest, with a population of over 21,000. Frankfort, Indiana, was actually founded and named in honor of the old home town on the Main, birthplace of a German pioneer named Benz, grandfather of the Pence brothers who owned the land on which the town's first building sprang up in 1826. By a meaningful coincidence, Frankfort, Indiana is the center of a large apple-growing region, though it leaves the dispensing of hard apple cider as a national beverage to its big brother across the Atlantic.

Information in the Frankfurt (Germany) city archives also includes mention of a number of other Frankfords and Frankforts. Unfurtunately, current population figures are not available, and in some cases the actual existance of the town is in question. It is probable that towns bearing the name have become incorporated into other communities and have lost their identity. It is suspected that in other cases, topographic features bearing the name have shown on some maps but not on others. Nonetheless, they are listed for interest's sake. If any reader should have further information concerning a town or other location bearing one of the forms of the name "Frankfurt", both the publisher and the director of the Frankfurt am Main city archives would be happy to receive such information. It is suggested that research centered around Frankforts in America would be a worthwhile project combining scholarship and field work for an amateur genealogist with plenty of time and travel expenses.

Among the local lore, he will discover choice historical tidbits, including the fact that America's entry into the Spanish-American War was announced at Frankfort, In-

STATE	CITY	POPULATION* (1970)
Kentucky	Frankfort	21,356
Indiana	Frankfort	14,956
Illinois	West Frankfort	8,836
New York	Frankfort	3,305
Illinois	Frankfort	2,325
Ontario	Frankford	1,862
Michigan	Frankfort	1,660
Kansas	Frankfort	960
Ohio	Frankfort	949
Delaware	Frankford	635
Missouri	Frankford	472
Maine	Frankfort	—
Illinois	Frankfort Heights	—
Tennessee	Frankfort	—
Alabama	Frankfort	—
Pennsylvania	Frankford Stadion, Philadelphia	—
South Dakota	Frankfort	—
West Virginia	Frankford	—
Pennsylvania	Frankford Arsenal	—
Missouri	New Frankfort	—

Also listed (from Frankfurt am Main archives and other sources):

Wisconsin	Frankford	
Iowa	Frankfort	
Texas	Frankford	
New Jersey	Frankfort	
New Jersey	Frankford Plains	
Minnesota	Frankford	
Ohio	Frankfort Corners	
Washington	Frankfort	
New York	Frankfort Hill	
Pennsylvania	Frankfort Springs	
Pennsylvania	Frankford Creek	
Indiana	New Frankfort	
Michigan	South Frankfort	

* Population figures from Rand McNally Road Atlas (1975).

192

diana by the booming of a home-made cannon, constructed from a bored-out locomotive axle. According to the Hoosier State Guide, the town's skyline is dominated by the clock tower of the old courthouse and the home office building of an insurance company.

Frankfurt high school principal Max Zimpel visited the Kyger School there in 1937 after a locally-publicized exchange of letters between his students and those of Frankfort, Indiana. Invited by the mayor and a committee of 60 leading citizens, Zimpel charmed his audience in a talk about the old home town to the point where a surprised Frankfurt mayor received a telegram the following day reading: 'After speech of Max Zimpel, citizens of Frankfort Indiana send heartiest greetings to mother city'.

In 1973 the U. S. Consul General of Frankfurt, Robert H. Harlan, wrote to the mayors of all the Frankforts in America, inviting them to participate in the Castle Festival of Hoechst (Hoechster Schlossfest), which that year was a joint German-American enterprise. The most enthusiastic response came from Frankfort, Illinois, which sent many items of current and historic interest for display in the 14th century castle at the Frankfurt suburb of Hoechst. The town also sent a delegation of some 50 loyal citizens to attend the festival. In a reciprocal gesture the following year, Buergermeister Rudi Soelch and several members of the city council visited Frankfort "off-the Main", on the plains of Illinois, enjoying a good dinner at the "Frankforter Hof" and the hospitality of the Frankfort citizens, many of whom are descendants of early settlers from the Frankfurt am Main area.

193

For the sake of historical accuracy, it must be recorded that the state capital of Kentucky was named Frankfort in 1786 by the city's founder, General James Wilkinson to perpetuate the memory of pioneer Steffen Frank who was shot by Indians. Some years earlier, fellow settlers had given his name to a river fording on the site of the new town. The way 'Frank's ford' evolved into 'Frankfort' in English paralleled developments a thousand years earlier when the name of the Main river metropolis evolved from a ford across the Main used by the tribe of the Franks — the Frank's ford.

Like Frankfort, Kentucky, most U. S. Frankforts were originally named after various 'Franks', in one case after the 'frankness' of early settlers. Canada too has a Frankford on Lake Ontario (pop. 1, 8, 62), and there is a profusion of South, West and New Frankforts; Frankfort Hill, Springs, Creek and Station thrown in for good measure, though the sum total of their populations is less than one tenth that of their older namesake across the Atlantic.

ARE DATES IMPORTANT?

Some of he dates in Frankfurt history, recorded below are significant, others less so. It will be up to the reader to decide which of them—if any—he wants to retain. The concurrent events in world history, listed alongside the Frankfurt dates, are just as meaningful, for they too were picked at random. You never can tell when they might come in handy on a quiz show and what new relations students in search of a thesis might establish between them.

194

WORLD HISTORY	FRANKFURT HISTORY
793 First Norman invasion of England	Documents first mention 'Franconofurd'
1152 Church of Ireland under jurisdiction of the Pope in Rome	Barbarossa (Red Beard) elected king
1330 Invention of the saw mill	King Ludwig the Bavarian grants permission to hold annual fair
1356 Renaissance starts in Italy	"Golden Bull" names city as the site of all future elections of German kings
1446 Explorer Diniz Fernandez sails as far as Cape Verde, Africa	Alderman submits expense accounts including visit in 'pleasure house' during official trip to Cologne
1525 Battle of Pavia, Charles V. defeats Frederick I of France	Frankfurt becomes Lutheran
1541 The Turks invade Hungary	E. Klein stands trial for hexing the milk of cow
1558 Accession of Elizabeth I of England to the throne	Protestants from Britain and the Netherlands find refuge in Frankfurt from religious persecution
1579 Circumnavigation of the globe by Sir Francis Drake, 1577-1580	Bankrupt businessmen are forced to wear yellow hats
1612 Founding of Nieuw Amsterdam, later known as New York	Revolt of small businessmen and artisans against the upper classes
1689 "Bill of Rights" establishes the Constitutional monarchy in England	First coffee house established in Frankfurt
1709 Russians defeat the Swedes at Poltava	Establishment of the first taxi stand; sedan chairs parked at the Hauptwache
1749 Christopher Gist sets out to explore the Ohio region	J. W. von Goethe born at Hirschgraben 23
1754 Benjamin Franklin makes a trip from Philadelphia to Portsmouth, N.H. in 18 days	Sour apple cider, later to become Frankfurt's national beverage, first on tap at Werner's garden restaurant in Sachsenhausen

WORLD HISTORY	FRANKFURT HISTORY
1762 Rousseau's "Contract social" published	First street lights installed; smoky oil lanterns
1764 Enraged mobs set fire to house of Massachussetts Lieutenant Governor Hutchinson	Anna Maria Setter is the name of a lady shot in the skirmish for a piece of the coronation ox roasted on the Roemerberg
1785 "The Times" first published in London	Frenchman J. P. Blanchard soars 6000 feet in balloon
1810 Cornelius Vanderbilt establishes ferry between Staten Island and New York City	Frankfurt becomes Grand Duchy under Napoleon's protection
1826 Discovery of ancient Greek culture exites Europe	Paper money issued in Frankfurt for the first time
1838 Coronation of Queen Victoria of England	Death of Herr Stilgebauer, last man to wear a powdered wig and pigtail in Frankfurt
1839 Process of vulcanizing rubber developed by Charles Goodyear	The Society for the Prevention of Cruelty to Animals invites to a horsemeat banquet in Bornheim. The horse died of natural causes after reaching a ripe old age
1845 Annexation of Texas	Frankfurt streets first lit by gaslight
1848 Revolutions sweep Europe	Revolutionary constitutional assembly meets in Frankfurt to draft constitution for a united Germany
1864 Karl Marx, founder of world communist movement organizes the 'First International'	Opening of the first two public comfort stations 'as an experiment'
1872 Pullman introduces the first dining car	First horse trolley takes off from Hauptwache at 10 mile clip
1881 Tsar Alexander II of Russia assassinated	Fifty wealthy Frankfurters become initial customers of the new telephone exchange
1914 Outbreak of First World War	Founding of Frankfurt University

INDEX